Beyond Fences

Seeking Social Sustainability in Conservation

The World Conservation Union

Biodiversity
Support
Program

WWF

USAID

The Nature Conservancy®

CIFOR

CENTER FOR INTERNATIONAL FORESTRY RESEARCH

CARE

WORLD LEARNING

This publication has been made possible in part by funding from the GTZ Protected Area Management Project.

Published by: IUCN, Gland, Switzerland and Cambridge, UK

                    First published 1997
                    Reprinted 2000

Citation: Borrini-Feyerabend, G.with Buchan, D. (ed.), 1997. *Beyond Fences: Seeking Social Sustainability in Conservation*. Vol. 1. IUCN, Gland, Switzerland and Cambridge, UK. v + 129 pp.

ISBN: 2-8317-0340-9

Cover design and   Fabrizio Prati
drawings:

Layout and design: Grazia Borrini-Feyerabend and Patricia Halladay

Printed by: Rosette Printers, Karachi, Pakistan

Available from: IUCN
                 Publications Services Unit
                 219c Huntingdon Road
                 Cambridge CB3 0DL
                 United Kingdom
                 Tel: + 44 1223 277894
                 Fax: + 44 1223 277175
                 E-mail: info@books.iucn.org
                 www.iucn.org/bookstore/index.html

                 A catalogue of IUCN publications is also available

Beyond Fences

Seeking Social Sustainability in Conservation

VOLUME 1:

A Process Companion

Edited by Grazia Borrini-Feyerabend

with Dianne Buchan

Acknowledgments

This publication is the result of a collaborative exercise and incorporates contributions from more than 100 people from over 20 countries. The names of these people and the roles they played are listed in the Contributors sections at the end of Volumes 1 and 2. The Biodiversity Support Program, the Social Policy and Resettlement Division of the World Bank, the PVO-NGO-NRMS project, the World Wildlife Fund-US, CIFOR and Intercooperation provided financial support to IUCN for implementing the project, and staff from these organizations — Janis Alcorn, Michael Brown, Gloria Davis, John Krijnen, Patricia Larson, Kathleen McPhail, and Eva Wollenberg — contributed ideas, contacts, and written materials to the editor and IUCN project manager — Grazia Borrini-Feyerabend — throughout the process. The IUCN Social Policy Group was able to manage the process thanks to the sponsorship of the Danish International Development Agency (DANIDA), which is gratefully acknowledged.

The project began with discussions between BSP and IUCN in mid-1994, which later involved other institutions interested in participating in a joint undertaking. The project was officially launched with professional staff from the sponsoring agencies establishing the Project Coordination Committee, which guided the project throughout, and with a workshop at IUCN headquarters in December 1994. On the basis of the workshop's results, the editor conceived the original design of organizing the work around key questions — focusing on processes and offering examples rather than creating a definitive book of answers — and produced a draft volume in the spring of 1995.

In the following months, the draft was reviewed by members of the Project Coordinating Committee and by many field-based professionals around the world, all of whom provided general and specific feedback. In particular, input was sought and received on the "options for action" and on experiences and examples that could illustrate their relevant benefits and drawbacks. The examples received are now listed in Volume 2, and the general input and comments have been incorporated throughout the text of the two volumes. Dianne Buchan, a consultant with the IUCN Social Policy Group, was in charge of much of this work.

While developing the first volume, a number of terms and concepts deserving some detailed illustration were identified. In the fall of 1995, experts on the relevant subjects were contacted and asked to write short papers on those topics, now included in the book as "concept files". These were further supplemented by a section on participatory tools and processes written by the editor and Dianne Buchan from their own personal experiences, existing literature and contributions received. In March 1996, the Project Coordinating Committee reviewed progress and provided further input to both volumes. A revised version was distributed to several independent reviewers in the summer of 1996. Their comments were integrated and further suggestions from the Coordinat-

ing Committee were added up to January 1997. The kindness and flexibility of Fabrizio Prati, illustrator, Patricia Halladay, designer, and Susan Broomfield, chief SPG secretary, were invaluable in the process.

The editor designed the structure and wrote some of the original draft texts, later commented upon by contributors. Other original drafts were written by members of the Coordinating Committee and later edited at IUCN. Sections without named authors are thus all a 'joint product' of various contributors and the editor.

I am sincerely grateful to all the people who contributed to Beyond Fences *for their generous and inspiring insights, their responsiveness to questions and their readiness to debate. Personally, I wish to dedicate this work to Tata, a woman who never learned to read or write, and yet knew extremely well how to deal with people, animals, plants and the land. May she inspire the users of these volumes to go beyond the written words.*

Grazia Borrini-Feyerabend
Gland, Switzerland, February 1997

Contents

Introduction

Why these resource books? 1

What will the books provide? 1

What will the books not provide? 2

Who are the books for? 2

What is a "conservation initiative"? 2

Using the resource books 3

Seeking social sustainability 11

Section 1: Involving the people

1.1   Involving the people 20

1.2   Key questions 22

1.3   Indicators of participation 32

1.4   Options for action 34

Section 2: Addressing local needs in conservation

2.1   Addressing local needs in conservation 56

2.2   Key questions 58

2.3   Indicators of local needs being addressed 68

2.4   Options for action 70

Section 3: Managing a sustainable initiative

3.1   Managing a sustainable initiative 94

3.2   Key questions 96

3.3   Indicators of sustainable internal management 102

3.4   Options for action 104

General References 118

Contributors 125

Volume 1

Contents

Volume 2

Section 4:Concept files

4.1   Social actors and stakeholders 3

4.2   Indigenous resource management systems 8

4.3   Local institutions for resource management 14

4.4   Population dynamics and conservation 17

4.5   Gender concerns in conservation...22

4.6   Participation in conservation: why, what, when, how? 26

4.7   Equity in conservation 32

4.8   Applied ethics in conservation...35

4.9   Biodiversity and rural livelihood...38

4.10   Local knowledge in conservation 41

4.11   Indigenous peoples and protected areas 44

4.12   Social concerns in population resettlement 50

4.13   Poverty, wealth and environmental degradation 55

4.14   Common property, communal property and
open access regimes 59

4.15   Conflicts in conservation 62

4.16   Collaborative management for conservation 65

4.17   Governance and the rule of law...68

4.18   Decentralizing and devolving government 70

4.19   Primary environmental care 74

4.20   Sustainable use of wildlife...79

4.21   Sustainable farming, forestry and fishing practices 82

4.22   Ecotourism 86

4.23   Compensation and substitution programmes.........................91

4.24   Jobs in conservation 94

4.25   Economic valuation in conservation.......................................96

4.26   Incentives and disincentives to conservation 100

4.27   A project or a process? 103

4.28   Management styles 107

4.29   Cross-cultural communication and local media....................111

4.30   Social sustainability 115

Section 5: Participatory tools and processes

5.1   Social Communication 121

        5.1.1   Community and public meetings 122

        5.1.2   Audio-visual presentations 124

        5.1.3   Picture stories (flip charts and flannel boards) 126

        5.1.4   Street or village theatre 128

        5.1.5   Radio programmes 129

5.2   Information gathering and assessment 130

        5.2.1   Natural group interviews 131

        5.2.2   Focus group interviews 132

        5.2.3   Semi-structured interviews with key informants 134

        5.2.4   Photo appraisal and slide language 135

        5.2.5   Observational walks and transect diagrams 136

        5.2.6   Trend analysis 137

        5.2.7   Land-use mapping 138

        5.2.8   Historical mapping 139

        5.2.9   Seasonal calendars 140

        5.2.10 Gender analysis 141

5.3   Planning 143

        5.3.1   Group brainstorming 144

        5.3.2   Guided imagery 145

        5.3.3   Problem and solution mapping 147

        5.3.4   Nominal group technique 148

        5.3.5   Ranking exercises 150

5.4   Conflict management 152

        5.4.1   A process for negotiation/mediation 153

5.5   Monitoring and evaluation 157

        5.5.1   Stakeholder accounts 158

        5.5.2   Community involvement to plan the evaluation 160

        5.5.3   Community-based environmental assessment 162

        5.5.4   SWOL analysis 163

5.6   References and further readings 165

Section 6: Examples from the field

Identifying stakeholders and informing them about the conservation initiative

6.1   Inventory of actual/potential stakeholders 171

6.2   Stakeholder analysis 173

6.3   Information campaign 174

6.4   Public relations service 176

6.5   Environmental discussion sessions 177

Building on the capacities of stakeholders and developing long-term relationships among them and the conservation initiative

6.6   Promoting internal discussion within each
        stakeholder group 180

6.7   Helping stakeholders organize 182

6.8   Meetings and workshops to build bridges among
        stakeholders 185

6.9   Visits to similar initiatives 186

6.10   Strengthening local institutions for resource management .. 188

6.11   Conservation Councils 189

6.12   Institution for conflict management 191

6.13   Training and incentives for staff 192

6.14   Promoting an effective legal basis for participation 194

Involving the stakeholders in the management of the conservation initiative

6.15   Assisting local communities to develop their own
        conservation initatives 195

6.16   Participatory appraisal and planning 198

6.17   Collaborative management agreement 203

6.18   Collaborative management institution 207

6.19   Devolving the initiative to local institutions 210

6.20   Participatory monitoring and evaluation 212

Understanding local management systems, local claims, needs and potential conservation impacts

6.21   Review of indigenous/customary systems 213

6.22   Participatory review of customary claims 215

6.23   Review of national policies and laws 216

6.24   Assessment of local uses of natural resources 219

6.25   Social impact assessment (SIA) 223

Planning to integrate conservation and the meeting of local needs

6.26 Open meetings among stakeholders 225

6.27 Special events and 'ideas fairs' 227

6.28 Visits to successful initiatives 229

6.29 Building upon local knowledge and skills 231

6.30 Participatory planning to integrate local needs 233

6.31 Zoning to separate incompatible land uses 236

Generating benefits for local stakeholders

6.32 Primary environmental care (PEC) projects 238

6.33 Jobs for local people 242

6.34 Local distribution of revenues 244

6.35 Compensation and substitution programmes 246

Enhancing the sustainability of benefits to stakeholders

6.36 Financial feasibility studies 248

6.37 Linking benefits with efforts in conservation 250

6.38 Supportive links with relevant services 251

6.39 Monitoring land tenure and land values 254

6.40 Incentives to conservation accountability 254

6.41 Biodiversity monitoring and surveillance by local people 256

6.42 Integrating initiatives with local empowerment 258

Improving internal relationships among staff and building upon their commitment and capacities

6.43 Staff review of internal management issues 259

6.44 Regular staff meetings 260

6.45 On-the-job capacity building 260

6.46 Decentralizing decision-making 262

6.47 Reviewing the initiative for timing and flexibility 264

Improving relationships among staff and local stakeholders

6.48 Hiring staff from the local area 264

6.49 Staff visits to the field operations 267

6.50 Cultural presentations for the staff of the initiative 267

6.51 Integrating local culture and traditions 269

Sustaining the relationship between the conservation initiative and local stakeholders

6.52 Extraordinary staff and stakeholder meetings 271

6.53 Ongoing communication programme 272

6.54 Monitoring change in local communities 273

6.55 Networking with local leaders and opinion-makers 274

References 276

Contributors 279

Natural resources are managed (or mismanaged) by people: individuals, families, groups, communities, associations, businesses and governments. To find out why an environment thrives or is exploited in a destructive way, find out about the people affecting it. Are they residents, regular transients, or one-time users of natural resources? How long have they been in the area? Are major changes happening in their societies? Do they feel a need to conserve their environment and resources? Do they know how to take care of them? Do they have the skills and means to do it? Do they get the support they need? Are there specific institutions in charge of managing the resources? Are there laws and rules about management? How many people use the resources? How healthy and wealthy are they? How secure do they feel? How do they share decisions and responsibilities? How do they deal with conflicting interests, in particular between local and external forces?

Even in specific conservation initiatives, such as the management of a protected area, it is very rare for the professionals in charge to be fully in control. In most cases, their interaction with society at large, and with local people in particular, is basic and inevitable. A variety of social actors and stakeholders shapes the legal, institutional, political and economic realities that affect the use of resources and the values assigned to them. Residents of local communities, in particular, possess precious knowledge and capacities, yet are too often ignored or humiliated in management processes. No wonder they become hostile to conservation initiatives that do not recognize their claims, and damage their interests.

There is little doubt that dealing with social concerns, particularly those of local communities, is essential for the success of conservation initiatives. Some governments and agencies express this by saying that there is a need to assure the social sustainability of such initiatives. In this sense, social sustainability depends on addressing the social, economic and cultural needs of the local communities — and stakeholders in general — affected by a conservation initiative, and on assuring the conditions (e.g., finances, technology, political authority and social organization and consensus) to maintain the conservation practices established.

How do we address such concerns? How do we make a conservation initiative socially sustainable? It is an assumption of our work that this cannot be done by experts in isolated offices, but requires the active participation of the stakeholders themselves — including the residents of local communities, often the least powerful and organized of them all. These resource books are designed to support a process by which such participation is achieved, a 'learning-by-doing' experience in which lessons are put into practice and people, together, find out what 'works' in their particular context.

Why these resource books?

What will the books provide?

These two volumes are designed to help professionals employed in conservation initiatives to identify the social concerns that are relevant for their work, assess options for action and implement the options best suited to their context.

The first volume is a companion to a process — an experience of 'learning-by-doing' expected to involve a series of meetings and field-based activities. The process may be carried out for the purpose of planning, evaluating or redesigning a conservation initiative.

The second volume contains a variety of reference material to be consulted, as needed, at various stages in the process.

What will the books not provide?

These resource books are not intended to offer 'the answers' to social concerns in conservation. They do not provide step-by-step instructions nor an all-purpose questionnaire. The questions, indicators and options for action listed in Volume 1 (the process companion) are not relevant in all contexts, and users will certainly think of more. The concept files, participatory tools and processes and examples provided in Volume 2 (the reference book) are offered as food for thought and do not constitute an exhaustive treatment of any subject.

Who are the books for?

Beyond Fences is written for professionals working in a conservation initiative. In the case of a protected area or state reserve, this usually means staff of national and local governments and agencies. In the case of a supporting project or programme, this may mean employees of a non-governmental organization (NGO), an aid agency or an international body. Thus, these resource books are for governmental or non-governmental staff, as well as for national or expatriate professionals. In particular, they address the managers of conservation initiatives and the professionals who interact with people and organized groups on a regular basis.

Beyond Fences can also be of help to professionals who are not field-based, but still involved in planning, financing and evaluating initiatives, and to various individuals and groups involved in conservation. Finally, it can be of utility in training environments for conservation professionals.

As a working definition employed in *Beyond Fences*, a conservation initiative is any medium- to long-term set of activities to maintain and protect natural environments and the quality of their biological diversity. In this sense, examples of a conservation initiative are the ongoing management of a protected area, the management of a territory under reserve status, or the management of a valuable ecosystem or species. All these may and usually do include forms of sustainable use of resources. Examples are also fixed-term projects or programmes providing support to the actors in charge of the above.

A conservation initiative generally applies to a territory with defined boundaries, and responsibility for its management is generally assigned to a specific institution. Besides such boundaries, however (e.g., the boundaries of a park), an initiative always has a broader area of influence. This area covers the territories where people are dependent — i.e., for food and income — on the natural resources the initiative aims to conserve. Sometimes these territories are referred to as "buffer zones". The area of influence also applies to the territories where economic or other types of human activities affect the resources to be conserved.

Given the work orientation of many of the individuals and institutions that developed *Beyond Fences* and are expected to use it, we will mostly deal with conservation initiatives in countries of the South (so-called developing countries).

What is a "conservation initiative"?

Beyond Fences is not meant to be read from cover to cover. The first volume is a companion to a process, and is meant to be used following the requirements of the process itself. It is not a guide and does not spell out step-by-step procedures. The second is a reference book, to be consulted on specific items as needs arise.

The volumes can be used by individuals, but they have really been designed for a team of professionals working together in a conservation initiative. The team should ideally include key managers as well as the staff responsible for the interaction with local people and organized groups. The resource books could be used by such a team at the beginning of an initiative as an aid to assess options and plan activities but they could also be helpful at later stages. In particular they could support various types of review, help to re-focus and redirect activities, and provide ideas to solve problems rooted in social issues. They could also serve as a basis for training personnel on social concerns in conservation.

We recommend that the team members who will use the books (let us call them the "professional team") familiarize themselves with the books' contents before doing anything else.

Volume 1 begins with some questions and answers on what the books are all about (you are reading that part right now). A brief introduction, entitled "Seeking social sustainability", discusses the reasons social concerns are important for a conservation initiative. The following three main sections address three such concerns: "Involving the people"; "Addressing local needs in conservation"; and "Managing a sustainable initiative". These three topics were identified by professionals with expertise in biological and social sciences and conservation prac-

Using the resource books

tice. They do not cover everything that is important about people and conservation, nor are they completely independent of each other. Yet, they group some major concerns and lessons on what motivates people to act for conservation, and what helps them succeed.

Volume 2 is also composed of three main sections. The first section, "Concept files", contains concise essays that illustrate key terms, concepts and considerations on particular conservation issues. The second section, "Participatory tools and processes", is useful for conservation professionals who wish to communicate with local people and involve them in gathering information, assessing problems and opportunities, planning activities, managing conflicts and monitoring and evaluating results. The third section is an extensive collection of brief examples from the field, offering lessons learned in conservation initiatives that seized or missed opportunities to take action on social concerns. This last section is closely linked to Volume 1, as it offers examples of what happens when the options for action listed in Volume 1 are actually put into practice or ignored.

Before we enter into specific suggestions on how to use the resource books, we also need to stress that they do not provide any general structure or framework to plan or review a conservation initiative. First, such a framework would need to include many more considerations than social concerns (e.g., matters of geopolitical opportunity or financial feasibility) which are well beyond the scope of this work. Second, specific frameworks are established and required practice for most institutions in charge of conservation initiatives (governmental agencies, aid agencies, NGOs) and each organization has its own guidelines and specific procedures. There is little value in trying to provide a generic model here. Third, and perhaps most important, even the organizations that in the past relied heavily on "project cycle" approaches are now exploring more flexible and loose alternatives (Cernea, 1996). The World Bank, for instance, is currently reassessing its procedures — from site identification to evaluation of activities — and discussing alternative modes of operation. The key verbs are now "listening", "confirming hypotheses", "exploring alternatives" and "learning-by-doing". The good judgement of staff and flexible, ongoing interaction with various social actors — not the strict application of rules and procedures — are beginning to be seen as central to the success of an initiative (Picciotto and Weaving, 1994).

How, then, can these resource books be used? The easy answer is that they should be used to support and complement whatever process the professional team in charge of the conservation initiative is already following — to plan, review, carry out training or evaluate its own work. The books can provide checklists and *aide memoires*, research questions and methods, ideas for activities to be tried out, themes for discussion in training sessions, possible indicators for monitoring and surveillance, and so on. They are not designed to 'guide' you to do anything, but instead offer for your attention and stimulate you to consider and discuss a wide menu of items and options (see Table 1).

Let us try to clarify this with more information on the content of Volume 1. Each of the three main sections of Volume 1 is structured in the same way. First, a series of key questions (and sub-questions) is introduced. These are meant to stimulate the professional team to discuss three sets of social concerns (i.e., participation, local needs and internal management) in the context of their particular initiative. The specific questions may be more or less relevant in different environments. Yet, a team that would meet around a table (or under a tree), answer the questions and discuss the answers, would explore much of what is important to know about those concerns in their specific context.

Not all the terms, concepts or issues will be familiar to everyone in the team. In that case, the concept files listed in Volume 2 may be useful; they are cross-referenced in Volume 1. You may want to take a look at those files if you are sufficiently intrigued or stimulated by some of the questions. It may also happen that some people in the team disagree on possible answers to a question. It is useful to acknowledge this early on, since people generally take for granted that others share their views and may end up discovering that this is not the case when it is too late to remedy. Most crucial, you may find out that you do not know the answers to some important questions. What could you do in that case?

Table 1

How to use the resource books (summary)

Process	Process companion (Volume 1)	Reference book (Volume 2)
Identify and discuss the social concerns relevant for the conservation initiative	Introductions and Key Questions (Sections 1.1; 1.2; 2.1; 2.2; 3.1; 3.2)	Concept files (Section 4)
If matters are not all clear and more information is needed, collect more	Indicators and warning flags (Sections 1.3; 2.3; 3.3)	Participatory tools and processes for information gathering and assessment (Section 5.2)
Discuss the supplementary information and compare the relative effectiveness, appropriateness to context, and feasibility of different options for action; plan how to incorporate the selected options in the conservation initiative	Options for action (Sections 1.4; 2.4; 3.4)	Examples from the field (Section 6) Participatory tools and processes for social communication, planning and conflict management (Sections 5.1; 5.3; 5.4)
Take action on social concerns by implementing the selected options as part of the conservation initiative; monitor and review the activities on an ongoing basis		Participatory tools and processes for monitoring and evaluation (Section 5.5)

You may want to read further along in Volume 1, where indicators and warning flags are listed for each set of concerns, and in Volume 2, where participatory tools and processes are illustrated. Finding out about social indicators and warning flags in a participatory way, directly involving the people you are dealing with, is an excellent way of both gathering information and improving social relations with the conservation initiative.

Once you are satisfied with answering questions and discussing particular social concerns, you may want to explore what can be done about them. Each section in Volume 1 moves from questions to indicators to options for action. The options are activities that respond to particular needs and could be incorporated in the plan of action of the conservation initiative. It is important to stress that not all options are appropriate in all contexts, and that several of those listed are, in fact, alternative choices. All options should be evaluated on a case-by-case basis, and especially in terms of the assumptions they hold true (implicitly or explicitly), the trade-offs they require and their feasibility in the local context.

When you have identified an option as potentially appropriate, you may want to find out more about it by reading about some examples from the field where the option has been utilized or ignored. Section 6 of Volume 2 encompasses a range of such examples, cross-referenced to Volume 1. In some cases, the reader is also referred to concept files and participatory tools and processes in Volume 2.

The three main sections in Volume 1 can be explored in any order. They can simply complement — in total or in part — the process of planning, review, evaluation or training that may be taking place in the conservation initiative. If the team members are designing a monitoring programme, for instance, they may first want to consider the three sets of indicators and warning flags included in Volume 1 and the methods and tools in Section 5.5. If they are having a refresher training session they may hold some meetings to discuss one or more key questions listed in Volume 1, or concept files from Volume 2. If the initiative is plagued by conflicts or missed opportunities, the team may wish to identify alternatives by reviewing the options for action listed in Volume 1 and the relevant examples from the field in Volume 2. If the initiative is being planned from scratch, the team may want to explore all the questions and options listed in Volume 1 and put to use the participatory methods and tools illustrated in Volume 2 to involve local people in the assessment and planning itself (see Table 1). Some concrete examples may help you visualize how something like this could work out in practice.

Community-based resource management in Central Africa

An integrated conservation and development project is being planned in Dense Forest in Bangassou in the Central African Republic (Telesis, 1996). UNDP and USAID are funding the design of the project, with technical support from the World Wildlife Fund and the Private Voluntary Organizations and Non-governmental Organizations in Natural Resources Management (PVO-NGO/NRMS) Project. The goal of the project is to enable the local people to manage their renewable resources in a sustainable way, and the project has to figure out how best could this be achieved, with particular attention to the policy environment, the local economy, and the existing knowledge, skills and institutions for the management of natural resources. The region encompasses primary and secondary forests at various stages of regeneration. It possesses significant species richness, including populations of large mammals fleeing intense hunting pressures in the Sudan. The region is very remote, with a small population and chronic economic stagnation.

The project is being designed on the basis of various hypotheses, including the following:
* that a reform of tenure laws and practices is a precondition for reversing destructive land uses;
* that the diversification of local employment can reduce pressures on threatened natural resources; and
* that local communities can effectively take control of local environmental management and conservation activities.

Project management is expected to be minimal, and most planning and management decisions are to be carried out by local communities.

The 'minimal' professional team working for this project could make use of the resource set in several ways. Since local participation is a crucial component of the project, they could first review Section 1 of Volume 1 as an aid to reflect upon the existing social reality and to identify which activities can be planned, and in what order. They could also review some concept files of particular concern to them, e.g., "Indigenous resource management systems", "Local institutions for resource management", "Social actors and stakeholders", "Decentralizing and devolving government", "Local knowledge in conservation" and "Cross-cultural communication and local media".

Once they have outlined a plan to involve the communities in the initiative, they could consider using some of the participatory methods and tools listed in Section 5 and developing a monitoring system that includes collecting data on some of the indicators listed in Section 1. As they progress, they may find that it becomes more and more important to assure that conservation and the meeting of local needs are pursued through the same activities. Section 2 of Volume 1 may then help by offering more ideas to be considered and discussed with the local people. In the discussions, the examples of Section 6 may be recalled, so that lessons learned in past successes and failures are shared and taken in.

Finally, some problems may at one time or another surface between the 'minimal' professional staff and the local people, or within the staff itself. It may then be the moment to review what Section 3 of Volume 1 has to offer, and possibly review the project management process on that basis.

Mitigation measures in Lao People's Republic

The World Bank has been asked to back up some major financial investments in the Lao People's Republic that would provide infrastructure work (damming an important watershed for the production of hydro-electric power). The artificial lake to be created would flood an area of rich biodiversity and deprive a number of local indigenous communities of their land and means of livelihood. Prior to making a decision on the matter, the Bank has commissioned an in-depth study of environmental and social impact. This is expected to be the basis of a plan for mitigation measures that would provide maximum protection for the integrity of local biodiversity and the interests of the local people. Short of scrapping the project plan — which seems highly unlikely in the current political context in Lao — the mitigation measures may help minimize ecological damages and assure that people affected are equitably treated and compensated.

In this context, *Beyond Fences* may help to provide for the social sustainability of any mitigation plan that may be initially developed. If, for instance, the plan foresees relocation and compensation for the affected people, team members may find useful insight in various concept files (e.g., "Social concerns in resettlement programmes", "Equity in conservation", "Compensation and substitution programmes", "Cross-cultural communication and local media", "Poverty, wealth and environmental degradation", "Population dynamics and conservation") and a series of ideas for local investments to link environmental conservation and local livelihood in Section 2 of Volume 1. As for the Central African case, the participatory methods and tools illustrated in Volume 2 may help involving the local communities in the planning of the mitigation activities.

Conserving Lake Victoria

The IUCN Office in Eastern Africa developed a project proposal for the conservation of natural resources in Lake Victoria (IUCN, 1996). This followed the rapid development of the fishing export industry, which had adversely affected the lake's environmental quality and biodiversity. The project seeks to promote sustainable use of the lake's resources and to examine how the interests of the traditional fisheries can be reconciled with those of the export-oriented fisheries. A preliminary analysis identified and analyzed a range of local stakeholders, including those directly linked with the industry, such as local fishermen, fishmongers, fish processors, local communities in general (as consumers and employees) and local NGOs. The challenge ahead is for the stakeholders to be fully engaged in planning and implementing activities that will lead to the effective conservation of the integrity and biodiversity of Lake Victoria's ecosystem and resources. The professional team in charge of the initiative is expected to be relatively large and may have to include representatives from several countries. It may become even larger as the team interacts with the numerous stakeholders who — following the explicit strategy of the programme — should be empowered to take action for the conservation of their environment.

How could the staff of the Lake Victoria conservation project make use of *Beyond Fences*? There are various ways. First of all, they may wish to use all they can find in the books to help them identify and contact stakeholders (e.g., the questions and options in Section 1). They may then direct their attention to developing resource management agreements involving the stakeholders: a matter that is still poorly documented in development and conservation literature to date.

Section 1 of Volume 1 contains several checklists to help review relevant information and numerous options for action that lead to management agreements, conflict resolution among stakeholders and — possibly — local institutions taking charge of management decisions in the long run. In Volume 2, more ideas and references on the subjects can be found in various concept files ("Conflicts in conservation", "Collaborative management regimes", "Equity in conservation", "Sustainable farming, forestry and fishing practices", "Incentives and disincentives to conservation", etc.), in Section 5 (Participatory tools and processes for planning and managing conflicts) and Section 6 (Examples from the Field).

The Lake Victoria programme specifies that staff of national institutions for resource management will be trained to interact effectively with local stakeholders and to involve them in conservation activities. *Beyond Fences* can also be used to support this component. If a problem-based (not a lecture-type) methodology is adopted, trainees should first identify some of the problems they have encountered in their interactions with various groups of stakeholders (fisherpeople, those employed in transportation and local industries, fish vendors, etc.). They could then go through the two resource books to identify what they could do to meet these challenges. They could, for instance, pick some options for action, discuss them in their work groups and take notes about the discussions. After training, the resource books would remain both a useful reminder of discussions and a collection of ideas.

PROBONA is a joint initiative of the Swiss NGO Intercooperation and the IUCN office for South America (SUR). The project is concerned with the conservation of native forests in the Andean region. It includes a review of the present status of relevant ecosystems, demonstration cases of sustainable use of forest resources, coordination of various social actors at both the level of general information and the level of practice, strengthening of regional capacity and applied research (IUCN, 1994). The projects run by Intercooperation usually pay great attention to monitoring both the planned activities and outputs and the socio-economic change that results. Projects usually last several years and are subject to review on a regular basis.

Monitoring conservation in South America

For a project such as PROBONA, *Beyond Fences* could be useful as a tool to review how social concerns are taken into consideration in the project itself. A meeting could be called among the project staff and various counterparts to illustrate the status of activities and identify problems. After the presentations, one possible course of action would be for the participants to split into three groups, each of which would explore issues of participation, needs and management. Groups would use the material in the resource set to identify key elements for reporting, prepare a summary of their analysis, and present it to the others.

Unlike Intercooperation, IUCN is a union of member organizations and is primarily interested in communicating and sharing knowledge among those members. Copies of *Beyond Fences* could be distributed to its members so that they can explore for themselves the crucial social issues that make a difference in their conservation work. Those issues could then be compared and discussed in workshops, where institution members of IUCN will have a common frame of reference and possibly even a common lexicon. For instance, the experience of PROBONA, summarized with the help of the resource books, could be presented as a case study for the others to discuss and build upon.

In Pakistan, Intercooperation is supporting several intermediate-level NGOs in the North West Frontier, Sindh and Punjab provinces. The emphasis is on promoting sustainable land-use practices (e.g., in forestry and agriculture) and on strengthening membership-based organizations. Although some of the partner NGOs are experienced in

Networking and capacity building in Pakistan and southern Africa

relating to local societies and achieving effective results with participatory methodologies, others are not.

Intercooperation could offer *Beyond Fences* as a tool for its partner NGOs. The resource books could be discussed in networking meetings and — when appropriate — tried out in field activities. Workshops could be called to discuss how the books can be used to plan, evaluate or redesign initiatives. Such workshops, in fact, may be scheduled as part of ongoing capacity-building.

Similarly, the volumes could be used in a six-week training course in Harare, promoted by IUCN and the Centre for Applied Social Sciences of the University of Zimbabwe. The course is a residential initiative in which mid-level natural resource managers from southern African countries gather to review the social concerns relevant in their work and identify ways to respond to them. *Beyond Fences* could be used by the course participants as a tool for group work, a source of ideas and/or a reference package.

We hope that these examples provide some ideas on how to use the resource books. Yet, we would like you to remember that social situations are invariably more complex than any document can fathom, and that local customs and language will be fundamental in shaping the way in which the matters outlined in these volumes will be understood and interpreted. In addition, it should not be expected that a positive compromise or 'happy ending' is achievable in all situations. Too often, power imbalances among stakeholders, human failures, lack of financial means, lack of accountability, natural disasters and the like will conspire against positive outcomes for both conservation and social concerns. Regular monitoring and feasibility assessments should be built into any initiative so that, at least, the professional team can quickly reassess actions, as needs arise.

Users of these volumes are strongly encouraged to incorporate other documents, resources and their own experience to build on the ideas and options offered here. *Beyond Fences* is intended to stimulate you to figure out what needs to be done and how it could best be done. It may look like a set of two books, but it isn't: *Beyond Fences* is a process!

References for introduction

Cernea, M., personal communication, 1996.

IUCN/SUR, Progress and Assessment Report 1994 of the Probona Project, Quito, 1994.

IUCN, Socio-Economics of the Nile Perch Fishery on Lake Victoria, Project Proposal, Eastern Africa Regional Programme of IUCN, Nairobi, 1996.

Picciotto R. and R. Weaving, "A new project cycle for the World Bank?" *Finance and Development*, Dec. 1994.

Telesis USA, Inc., Sustainable Economic Development Options for the Dzanga-Sangha Reserve (Central African Republic), Executive Summary, Providence R.I., 1996.

Why should conservation professionals be concerned about social issues? Why should they know about them and attempt to deal with them in a positive manner? The experiences of the past provide us with some possible answers.

Seeking Social Sustainability

Why incorporate social concerns in conservation?

Social acceptance is crucial for conservation to be sustainable. People play many direct and indirect roles in resource management. These roles need to be recognized and worked with in an effective manner. State policing and control against people's values and practices can work only to a point, especially under the mounting problems of poverty and population dynamics, and within a process of economic globalization. If people value and appreciate biodiversity, if organized groups derive concrete benefits from it, they have the best chances to succeed in conserving it in the long run. If they do not, they are likely to become their own worst enemies when state control is — for any reason — lessened. Conversely, experience shows a positive correlation between effective conservation and the provision of a wide range of social benefits and positive responses to social concerns.

The costs of top-down approaches are staggering. Has anyone ever added up the costs of imposed development and conservation initiatives in recent decades? All over the world, examples abound of top-down plans — concocted in faraway offices and totally impervious to local capacities and concerns — which absorbed huge resources for their design and implementation and evolved into enormous failures. Few governments can today afford the economic costs of imposed conservation (e.g., for fences and guards) or its political costs (civil disorders, negative public relations).

The benefits of collaborative approaches are there to be realized. Very few conservation agencies, however capable and well equipped, possess the capacities and comparative advantages necessary for the long-term sustainable management of natural resources. A variety of social groups, both local and non-local, can help, providing knowledge, skills and resources and carrying out tasks for which they are uniquely suited. For instance, state agencies can rarely do better than local communities in surveying the access to a protected area or detecting early warnings of fire. Experienced entrepreneurs with foreign connections are generally most effective in initiating a tourism business. Resource users possess detailed knowledge of local biodiversity and can be effective in monitoring it and suggesting how to preserve it locally. Importantly, they are often the most determined defenders of local resources against exploitation by external interests. Complementary capacities do exist; the challenge is to create the conditions for collaboration rather than competition and hostility.

Philosophies and practices have changed, with less money, new partners, new ideas. About 20 years ago governments and the donor community were generally ready to finance major development and conservation initiatives run by line ministries and national agencies. Today, the huge projects of the past are much less in favour, and the work of line ministries is increasingly being integrated with that of NGOs and communities. Even in protected area management, alternative approaches involving the contribution of NGOs and local groups are becoming commonplace (Poff, 1996). All this goes hand-in-hand with financial constraints caused by adjustment measures and decreasing donor budgets. In all, the number of large, top-down conservation projects to be implemented in the future is fast decreasing.

Effective processes and tools for socially sustainable conservation initiatives do exist and do work. In a variety of contexts, there have been positive results from approaches that respond to the capacities and interests of local stakeholders and involve them in planning and implementing activities (see, for instance: Poffenberger 1990a and 1990b; West and Brechin, 1991; Geoghegan and Barzetti, 1992; Makombe, 1993; White et al., 1994; Western and Wright 1995; Weber 1995; Poffenberger, 1996). Moving from top-down approaches to participatory ones has promoted obvious and at times dramatic improvements in local environmental management and biodiversity conservation. In some cases the solution of local conflicts has been the basis for change. In others, a shift in the distribution of costs and benefits of conservation has made the difference. Change also comes as a result of developing specific agreements and appointing appropriate institutions for resource management.

Every initiative that affects people in a significant way involves a clear political and moral responsibility. Conservation is about managing natural resources — a topic with profound political implications, affecting people in important and multiple ways. As with any other endeavour that affects people, conservation cannot escape the responsibility of determining its consequences, as well as who will benefit from it and who will pay the costs. It is politically and morally unacceptable that in too many instances such responsibility is forgotten or shrugged off. In the long run this will only lead to bad social relationships and unsustainable initiatives.

Past Approaches

Most colonial and post-colonial approaches to conservation operated on the premise that local peoples' stakes and rights in natural resources were subsidiary to those of the state. State control over resource management was placed in the hands of technical elites and issues pertaining to social sustainability were of marginal concern at best. In particular it was often assumed that indigenous peoples were inimical to the conservation of wildlife and natural resources.

While one must be careful not to romanticize complex and evolving social realities, it cannot be denied that most traditional societies historically coexisted with biodiversity, and that cultures and people's production systems were often grounded in utilizing wild resources on a sustainable basis (see, for instance Turnbull, 1961 and 1972; Reader, 1988). Yet, throughout the past two centuries, traditional cultures and people were perceived by conservation planners mainly as threats. They were not involved in deciding how to manage resources; on the contrary, they were commonly ordered out of their territories and deprived of access to the natural basis of their livelihood without discussion or compensation. These potential stewards of biodiversity were alienated from conservation, often to the point of becoming its active opponents.

As an example, African traditional hunters were branded as 'poachers' and pastoral peoples — such as the Maasai — were perceived as one of the major threats to wildlife. The fact that the big game dear to conservationists coexisted for centuries with these pastoral populations did not seem to correct that perception. As aptly described by Adams and McShane (1992):

"The method for establishing parks has hardly changed in over a century. The process has always involved the expensive operation of removing those people living on the newly protected land. In almost all cases, the result is a park surrounded by people who were excluded from the planning of the area, do not understand its purpose, derive little or no benefit from the money poured into its creation, and hence do not support its existence. As a result, local communities develop a lasting distrust of park authorities, in part because of the glaring lack of attention those authorities, supported by conservationists, have traditionally paid to the link between park ecology, the survival of wildlife, and the livelihood of displaced people."

Fortunately, conservation is evolving. On the one hand, it is improving its scientific understanding of human beings as components of ecosystems and moving away from an exclusive focus on the scientific aspect of biodiversity towards a better understanding and appreciation of its economic and cultural values. On the other, conservation is expanding its practice to include — besides traditional protected area management skills — a variety of participatory approaches, new institutions and multiple/sustainable use schemes.

New approaches

The first aspect of this change, which could be termed "socio-biological", greatly profited from scientific advances in ecosystem and species management. As an example, "gap analysis" now determines where gaps in biodiversity exist and need to be filled for the benefit of larger ecosystems (Primack, 1995). An application of this understanding recently promoted the survival of endangered bird species in Hawaii. In general, management plans are now much more concerned with ecosystem resilience, as is the case with the plans of the Pantanal in Brazil, Bolivia and Paraguay. Landscape conservation, the potential human utilization of biodiversity and the existing policy and institutional environment are also acquiring greater importance in ecosystem management, as exemplified by some recent assessments of terrestrial ecoregions in Latin America and the Caribbean (BSP et al., 1995; Dinerstein et al., 1995). In all, the role humans play in shaping ecosystems is becoming better known. In coming years, it is likely that such a role will be integrated in more sophisticated ways in the management of ecosystems, to accommodate acceptable levels of resource use on a case-by-case manner.

In terms of protected areas, 'paper parks' disjointed from local societies and decided solely on the basis of donor funding are — it is hoped — a feature of the past (Barzetti, 1993). Site selection for protected areas is increasingly based on considerations of both biological value and social feasibility (Amend and Amend, 1995). Increasingly, conservation and development priorities are being integrated in strategies and plans (Brown and Wyckoff-Baird, 1994; Wells and Brandon, 1994; Vane-Wright, 1996). Studies are carried out to estimate the economic value of biodiversity in specific territories (WWF, 1995) and to understand the conditions in which community-based conservation develops and flourishes (Pye-Smith et al., 1994; Western and Wright, 1995). And in-depth understanding is sought as to how the commercial utilization of wild species promotes or detracts from conservation (Freese et al., 1994).

The second aspect of the evolution of conservation could be called "methodological-institutional". The key questions are: what means, processes and institutions render conservation feasible, effective and sustainable? No general answers can be provided to these questions, but resources such as *Beyond Fences* can facilitate the extensive context-specific inquiry necessary to provide local answers. If something general can be said it is that conservation is a complex matter, involving a variety of perceptions and interests. At best, all such perceptions and interests meet in designing and implementing plans and activities. Polarized views — such as that "conservation is only a by-product of a development agenda" or that "conservation is only a matter of sound biological science" — contribute very little to real initiatives on the ground. What is important, however, is to recognize that all conservation initiatives need to be accountable to somebody, and that local communities are among the first to whom they should be accountable.

Increasingly, a variety of social groups are called on to contribute to conservation efforts and receive benefits in return (McNeely, 1995; Ghimire and Pimbert, 1996; Borrini-Feyerabend, 1996). Such benefits may be economic, such as access to resources, or the sharing of revenues in various private and public ventures (e.g., park fees, hunting trophies, tourist enterprises, etc.). Or they may be cultural, such as the respect of local sacred sites, or the simple recognition of local communities as the rightful stewards of local resources. The theory is very simple: conservation is sustainable when, for all the relevant parties, its benefits are greater than its costs. In practice, attaining this condition is invariably difficult. At times, even striking a balance between conservation and local needs does not appear possible. In those cases a conservation initiative should make the trade-offs very clear, make sure that the appropriate authorities and stakeholders are aware and involved, and support equitable solutions.

Social Sustainability

It is not our intention to provide a seamless definition of social sustainability in conservation. On the contrary, we would like to explore the concept in a broad way, starting from a variety of meanings usually associated with it. Among these are the following:

- the maintenance or improvement of people's well-being over time, based on an equitable distribution of costs and benefits of production systems;
- the presence of resource management systems that allow for the regeneration or replenishment of the resource base over time, which will in turn depend on the resilience of a particular ecosystem; and
- the inter-generational compromise by which present resource users can guarantee future generations the right to a similar resource base and lifestyle.

The above involve several considerations, whose relative weight can only be judged within a specific context. Among others, these considerations include:

- the security of access to resources and the security of tenure, as the livelihood of many rural populations depends on them and on the overall health of the natural resource base;
- the range of economic opportunities offered by the natural resources, both to local populations and outside actors;
- the local institutional capacity for resource management;
- the local system of governance, rule of law and respect for justice, including the traditional and customary law and resource management systems;

- the recognition of the range of stakeholders involved in or vying for the resources included in conservation initiatives; and
- the local and non-local conditions that allow for constructive dialogue and negotiation between a wide variety of actors and external factors (market, political and institutional climate, etc.) and, in particular, for giving voice to people affected by conservation initiatives and who too often do not have the power to affect them.

It is crucial to achieve a balance between the biological concerns of conservation and the socio-economic and equity concerns of the people involved. Innovative approaches are being carried out, but critical gaps and unanswered questions still exist. These resource books have been developed to help achieve such a balance in specific conservation initiatives. The people and institutions which contributed to develop them are aware that no general answers or step-by-step guidelines can be provided to the professionals involved in conservation. Yet, there are meaningful questions, ideas, options, lessons from the past, concepts, tools and processes that can help. Some of these have been gathered in these two volumes.

The challenges ahead

Some questions, in particular, appear crucial to conservation and spell out the challenges for the future in every specific site and territory. Among these are the following:

- **Can conservation find roots in local and indigenous knowledge and institutions?** Can it benefit both the environment and the cultural identity of local societies? Are local knowledge and institutions open to integrate non-local lessons and positive contributions?

- **Who are the legitimate stakeholders in a given territory or set of resources?** Can they all afford to participate in conservation? Are they organized to represent themselves? Can they contribute to conservation and receive benefits from it?

- **Can the stakeholders enter into a partnership for conservation?** What criteria can best guide such a partnership and the sharing of relevant rights and responsibilities in resource management?

- **Is anyone promoting a process of communication, negotiation and conflict management among stakeholders?** Can the stakeholders develop an appropriate institution to be in charge of resource management and respond to the changing needs of the relevant ecosystems and people?

- **Are there effective options for local stakeholders to meet their needs (livelihood as well as cultural and identity needs) alongside conservation or — ideally — because of it?** Are the existing legal, and institutional conditions — for instance the national system of resource tenure and institutional recognition — geared for this to happen? Are the existing economic conditions — for instance, infrastructure, markets, credit and taxation systems — geared for this to happen?

In many ways, seeking social sustainability means seeking practical answers to these questions.

References

Adams, J. S. and T. O. McShane, *The Myth of Wild Africa: Conservation Without Illusion*, W. W. Norton and Co., New York, 1992.

Amend, S. and T. Amend, *National Parks Without People? The South American Experience*, IUCN, Gland (Switzerland), 1995 (also available in Spanish: *?Espacios sin Habitantes? Parques Nacionales de América del Sur*, IUCN Gland (Switzerland) and Nueva Sociedad, Caracas, 1992).

Barzetti, V. (ed.), *Parks and Progress,* IUCN, Gland (Switzerland), 1993.

BSP (Biodiversity Support Program), Conservation International, The Nature Conservancy, Wildlife Conservation Society, World Resources Institute and World Wildlife Fund, *Regional Analysis of Geographic Priorities for Biodiversity Conservation in Latin America and the Caribbean,* Biodiversity Support Program, Washington D.C., 1995.

Borrini-Feyerabend, G., *Collaborative Management of Protected Areas: Tailoring the Approach to the Context*, Issues in Social Policy, IUCN Gland (Switzerland), 1996.

Brown, M. and B. Wyckoff-Baird, *Designing Integrated Conservation and Development Projects*, Biodiversity Support Program with PVO-NGO/NRMS and World Wildlife Fund, Washington D.C., 1994.

Dinerstein, E. et al., *A Conservation Assessment of the Terrestrial Ecoregions of Latin America and the Carribean,* World Bank, Washington D.C., 1995.

Freese, C. et al., *The Commercial, Consumptive Use of Wild Species: Implications for Biodiversity Conservation*, World Wide Fund For Nature, Gland (Switzerland), 1994.

Geoghegan, T. and V. Barzetti (eds.), *Protected Areas and Community Management*, 'Community and The Environment — Lessons from the Caribbean', Series Paper 1, Panos Institute and CANARI (Caribbean Natural Resources Institute), Washington D.C., 1992.

Ghimire, K. and M. Pimbert., *Social Change and Conservation*, UNRISD, Geneva, 1996 (in press).

Makombe, K., *Sharing the Land*, IUCN/ROSA Environmental Issues Series, 1, Harare, 1993.

McNeely, J. A. (ed.), *Expanding Partnerships in Conservation*, Island Press, Washington D.C., 1995.

Poff, C., *Survey of Management Approaches in Protected Areas*, IUCN, Gland (Switzerland), 1996 (unpublished).

Poffenberger, M., "Conclusions: Steps towards establishing collaborative management", in Poffenberger, M. (ed.), *Keepers of the Forest*, Kumarian Press, West Hartford, 1990a.

Poffenberger, M., *Joint Management of Forest Land: Experiences from South Asia*, Ford Foundation, New Delhi, 1990b.

Poffenberger, M. and B. McGean (eds.), *Village Voices, Forest Choices*, Oxford University Press, New Delhi, 1996.

Primack, R., *A Primer of Conservation Biology*, Sinauer Associates, Sunderland, Massachusetts, 1995.

Pye-Smith, C. and G. Borrini-Feyerabend with R. Sandbrook, *The Wealth of Communities*, Earthscan, London, 1994.

Reader, J., *Man on Earth*, Penguin, London, 1990.

Turnbull, C., *The Forest People*, Simon and Schuster, New York, 1961.

Turnbull, C., *The Mountain People*, Simon and Schuster, New York, 1961.

Vane-Wright, R. I., "Identifying priorities for the conservation of biodiversity: systematic biological criteria within a socio-political framework" in Gaston, K. (ed.), *Biodiversity: A Biology of Numbers and Differences*, Blackwell, London, 1996.

Weber, J., "L'occupation humaine des aires protegées à Madagascar: diagnostic et éléments pour une gestion viable", *Natures, Sciences, Sociétés*, 3, 2: 157-164, 1995.

Wells, M. and K. Brandon, *People and Parks: Linking Protected Area Management with Local Communities*, World Bank, Washington D.C., 1994.

West, P. and S. R. Brechin (eds.), *Resident Peoples and National Parks*, University of Arizona Press, Tucson, Arizona, 1991.

Western, D. and R. M. Wright (eds.), *Natural Connections: Perspectives in Community-based Conservation*, Island Press, Washington D.C., 1995.

White, A. T., Hale-Zeitlin, L., Renard, Y. and L. Cortesi, *Collaborative and Community-based Management of Coral Reefs: Lessons from Experience*, Kumarian Press, West Hartford (Connecticut), 1994.

WWF (World Wide Fund for Nature), *Real Value for Nature: An Overview of Global Efforts to Achieve True Measures of Economic Progress*, WWF, Gland (Switzerland), 1995.

Section 1
Involving the people

"They think they created this World Heritage site by filling out a bunch of papers and encircling this area on a map! They didn't create it.... This forest and these animals wouldn't be here if we hadn't kept others out. We took care of this forest that our ancestors left us. We Karen are responsible for creating this World Heritage site, not the conservationists."

Village Headman, Thung Yai, Thailand, 1993

1.1

Involving the people

This section considers the prospects and methods for participation in practice. It helps the management team to answer the questions: "how do we involve the relevant people in the conservation initiative?" and "how do we get the stakeholders to participate?".

The team may find it helpful to visualize the degree of participation by locating it along a continuum (see Figure 1). At one end is the classic conservation project, which is controlled and run by specialists (national and/or expatriates), excludes the consideration of social concerns and various existing capacities, and does not involve stakeholders either in decisions or activities. At the other end are initiatives originated and fully controlled by stakeholders (e.g., communities, user groups, associations, private owners) with no interference from the agencies supposedly in charge. In between these extremes are various models of shared control that present different opportunities for and degrees of stakeholder participation.

Three main observations can be made. First: the location in Figure 1 (the actual *de facto* sharing of control) may not be sanctioned by law or policy (*de jure*). Control can be exercised in many ways, not all necessarily codified or explicitly mandated.

Second: stakeholder participation in an initiative has to be tailored to fit the unique needs and opportunities of each context. In other words, there is no 'best' place to be in the participation continuum. Different approaches should always be compared in terms of benefits, costs and expected effectiveness. A conservation initiative needs to find its appropriate niche in a specific historical and socio-political context and it is within that context that it should be evaluated.

Third: no matter where in the continuum a conservation initiative is 'born' or 'set', its position may change. For instance, changes in legal, political, socio-economic and ecological factors induce modifications in institutional settings and/or management practices, and they in turn affect the prospects (and needs) for stakeholder participation. In addition, facing concrete problems and 'learning-by-doing' often lead to a better recognition of the opportunity to involve various groups, particularly local people, in conservation.

Stakeholder participation presents different characteristics from place to place and it usually varies, even within a specific place, over time. A general consideration applies to all cases, however. Any initiative that wishes to respond positively to social concerns has to assume a conscious philosophy and approach. In other words, it has to be specific about who is expected to participate in what activities, and about why, how, when and under what conditions. This first section of Volume 1 helps the team to define the existing conditions for participation and to modify, accept or reject some specific options for action. In this sense, the scale at which the initiative operates is crucial. Activities that are feasible when dealing with a few communities may face serious constraints in time and budget when there is a large number of stakeholders.

The professional team should foresee a number of difficulties and be prepared to face them. While a conservation initiative that encourages participation is likely to benefit from the new approach, it is also likely to face new issues and dilemmas as a result of the involvement of various groups and individuals.

Figure 1

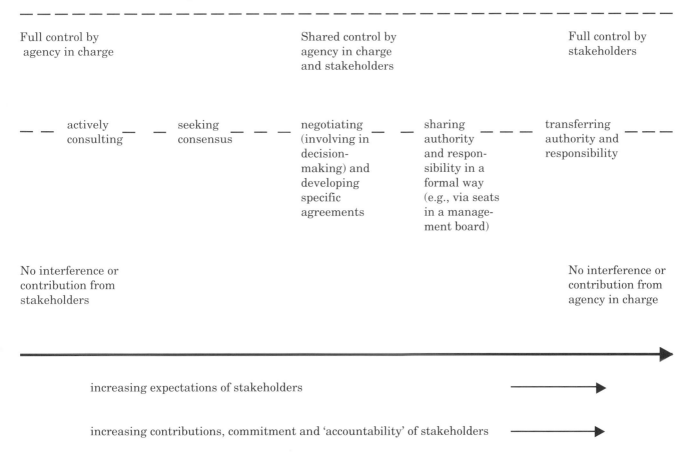

Participation in a conservation initiative: a continuum

Full control by
  agency in charge

Shared control by
agency in charge
and stakeholders

Full control by
stakeholders

actively
consulting

seeking
consensus

negotiating
(involving in
decision-
making) and
developing
specific
agreements

sharing
authority
and respon-
sibility in a
formal way
(e.g., via seats
in a manage-
ment board)

transferring
authority and
responsibility

No interference or
contribution from
stakeholders

No interference or
contribution from
agency in charge

increasing expectations of stakeholders

increasing contributions, commitment and 'accountability' of stakeholders

1.2

Key Questions

Key question 1.2.1

So far, who participates in the conservation initiative?

• Who had the idea of the initiative?

• Who is funding it?

• Who is (was) involved in planning it? Who actually worked on a management plan if one exists? Who made the major decisions about it?

• Who is responsible for implementing the initiative? Who is responsible for monitoring and evaluating it?

• Who knows and is regularly kept informed about the initiative and its functioning?

• So far, who has taken action for the initiative? Who has provided resources (human or otherwise)? Who has acquired benefits or suffered damages?

• Have some individuals or groups complained because they have not been informed, contacted, heard, involved or because they have been treated unfairly, have not received benefits, etc.?

• Is there any obvious social bias in terms of who has participated so far? For instance, have women, ethnic minorities, economically disadvantaged groups and various age groups been equitably involved in the initiative?

For further reference

Concept Files, Volume 2

Participation: why, what, when, how?
Social actors and stakeholders
Gender concerns in conservation
Indigenous peoples and protected areas
Local institutions for resource management
Equity in conservation

Who are the main stakeholders?

Key question 1.2.2

• Who are the people and groups actually or potentially affected by and/ or concerned about the conservation initiative? Are there: historic occupants, e.g., indigenous residents and regular transients? Local settlers who were already in the area before the beginning of the initiative? Recent migrants? Non-resident users of resources? Absentee landlords? Major secondary users (e.g., buyers of products, tourists)? Government agencies responsible for various resources? Local authorities? Local and national politicians? Interested NGOs, peoples' associations, research institutions, staff of relevant development and conservation projects? Interested businesses and industries?

• How are the natural resources to be conserved being used at present and by whom? Who specifically is having an impact on conservation? Has this changed over time?

• Who are the people or groups most dependent on the resources at stake? Is this a matter of livelihood or economic advantage? Are these resources replaceable by other resources not in the conservation area?

• Who possesses claims — including legal jurisdiction and customary use — over the resources at stake? Are several government sectors and ministry departments involved? Are there national and/or international bodies involved because of specific laws or treaties?

• Who are the people or groups most knowledgeable about, and capable of dealing with, the resources at stake? Prior to the conservation initiative, who was managing the resources? With what results?

• Are the stakeholders — and the stakeholders' interests in the resources — geographically and seasonally stable (e.g., are there seasonal migration patterns)? Are there major events or trends currently affecting the stakeholders (e.g., development initiatives, land reforms, migration, population growth or decline in a specific area, etc.)?

• Has there been a similar initiative in the region? If so, to what extent did it succeed? Who was in charge and how did local people respond?

Concept Files, Volume 2

Social actors and stakeholders
Biodiversity and rural livelihood
Indigenous resource management systems
Indigenous peoples and protected areas
Gender concerns in conservation
Population dynamics and conservation
Social concerns in resettlement programmes
Common property, communal property and open access regimes

For further reference

Key question 1.2.3

Are all stakeholders able to participate?

• Are there social factors (e.g., literacy, gender, ethnicity) affecting the ability of one or more stakeholders to contribute to and/or benefit from the conservation initiative?

• Do any of the venues used for meetings exclude a particular group (e.g., women, ethnic or religious group)? Is the language of meetings comprehensible to all?

• Can all stakeholders afford to participate (e.g., can they afford the time and/or expenses to reach a meeting venue)?

• Do all stakeholders feel comfortable participating (e.g., or are are they concerned about being asked for contributions they cannot make; do they fear being singled out or punished if they express themselves freely)?

For further reference

Concept Files, Volume 2

Participation: why, what, when and how
Social actors and stakeholders
Gender concerns in conservation
Poverty, wealth and environmental degradation
Governance and the rule of law

How do stakeholders relate to one another?

Key question 1.2.4

• Are there relationships of hierarchy or direct dependence among stakeholders? Are there powerful families, clans or businesses capable of influencing and controlling others? Is their power base stable or changing?

• Are there factions or political groups that separate and/or cut across stakeholders in the conservation initiative?

• What degree of autonomy do villages have? Do they collect taxes and use tax revenues to support local development, or are incomes being taxed to benefit others?

• Are the stakeholders' interests in the natural resources compatible with one another or in conflict? If conflicts of interest exist, is violence involved? Have the less powerful groups developed strategies to deal with those conflicts? Is the conservation initiative affecting these strategies? Is the initiative allied (or seen as being allied) with some parties in conflict with others?

• Are the local conflicts muddled or clear to all? Are conflicting parties discussing matters with one another? Is anyone facilitating the discussion? Are there local mechanisms and institutions which can help to mediate an agreement among them?

• Was there ever an agreement developed among conflicting parties (with or without external support)? If yes, how was it achieved?

• Have the stakeholders any previous experience of working together? If so, to what effect?

Concept Files, Volume 2

Social actors and stakeholders
Indigenous peoples and protected areas
Indigenous resource management systems
Conflicts in conservation
Equity in conservation
Decentralizing and devolving government

For further reference

Key question 1.2.5

Are all the stakeholders organized?

• Are there local institutions for resource management? How do they operate? With what results? Are they affected by the conservation initiative? Are they, or are they expected to be, involved in it in any positive way?

• Are all stakeholders organized in traditional institutions (e.g., clans), or official associations, with members, rules, etc.? Alternatively, are they organized informally or on an *ad hoc* basis, just for a specific purpose? Are any of them not organized at all?

• Does a suitable system of representation exist for all important stakeholders, so that they can play an active role in the conservation initiative?

• If representation exists, is it legitimate and accountable to all the relevant people? Is there any evident skewing in ethnic group, caste, age, class, gender or focus of interest among the representatives?

• If no suitable systems of representation exist, can something be done to help the stakeholders organize and interact with others?

• Has any stakeholder discussed the possibility of taking on some specific responsibilities in the management of the resources at stake?

For further reference

Concept Files, Volume 2

Social actors and stakeholders
Participation: why, what, when and how?
Local institutions for resource management
Indigenous resource management systems
A project or a process?

Have all the stakeholders been informed and been heard about the conservation initiative?

Key question 1.2.6

• Is the professional team working for the conservation initiative in touch with the local stakeholders? With all of them? At the appropriate level (e.g., at the level where people take and carry out decisions affecting natural resources)?

• Were/are the stakeholders contacted, informed and listened to in ways appropriate to their culture and level of literacy?

• Are all the stakeholders well-informed about the implications of the conservation initiative, i.e., knowledgeable about the specific benefits and costs actually or potentially accruing to them?

• Are the management and staff of the conservation initiative aware of what various stakeholders feel, believe and are doing about the initiative?

• Are some stakeholders collaborating with the conservation initiative? How did the collaboration develop?

• Are some stakeholders actively opposed to the conservation initiative? How does the opposition manifest itself?

Concept Files, Volume 2

Participation: why, what, when, how?
Social actors and stakeholders
Gender concerns in conservation
Conflicts in conservation
Local knowledge in conservation
Cross-cultural communication and local media

For further reference

Key question 1.2.7

Is there political support for participation in the conservation initiative?

• What is the political history of the area? Do local residents enjoy a degree of autonomy from the national government? For instance are local taxes used directly — at least in part — for local projects and benefits?

• What is the local experience of participation? Is there any history of political conflict associated with colonial, recent or contemporary regimes? Are people usually confident or fearful in expressing their opinions?

• Within the conservation community at local, national and international (e.g., donors) level, is there support for a participatory approach in the initiative at stake?

• What is the national government's attitude towards people's participation? Is the concept mentioned often or generally avoided? Is it used as a slogan? Is it practised in restrictive ways? Is participation ever repressed outright? Is it promoted and implemented in specific governmental sectors (e.g., the health system)? If yes, are there lessons learned there that can be of use in the conservation initiative?

• What is the attitude of the local government administration towards people's participation? Are local people usually informed and consulted about important decisions? Are they involved in development activities? In general, is the contribution of local people and groups recognized and valued by the local administration?

• Is people's participation in the conservation initiative likely to affect the distribution of power in the local area? If so, how are those adversely affected likely to respond? Are there individuals or groups (e.g., a major land-owner or armed resistance group) who may feel free to act outside legal constraints and affect people's participation in the initiative?

For further reference

Concept Files, Volume 2

Participation: why, what, when, how?
Gender concerns in conservation
Local institutions for resource management
Equity in conservation
Indigenous peoples and protected areas
Governance and the rule of law
Decentralizing and devolving government

Is there a legal and institutional environment favourable to participation?

• Is there a national or regional strategy for conservation? Does it make provision for recognizing local interests and capacities?

• Does the law recognize local actors (such as organized groups of resource users) as entities with legal status, the capacity to assume responsibilities, and the capacity to acquire benefits and share them among their members?

• Where stakeholders are involved, are they given equitable representation and 'weight' in the discussion and negotiation processes?

• What types of local institutions for resource management are officially recognized in the country? Are these also present at the site of the conservation initiative? If not, are they at least known by the local people?

• Are there — in the country or locally — peoples' associations and NGOs that could play a role for the conservation initiative? Are they known by the locals? Do they have any vested interests which could affect their acceptance by the local actors?

• Is the central government effectively sharing authority and responsibility with its regional, district and local representatives? Is there any specific legislation regulating such a "decentralization" process? Is that legislation actually implemented?

• In general, are policies and laws implemented and respected in the country? Is there a fair judicial system in place? Do people know and trust the system? Are there social pressures by which people feel bound to comply with norms, rules and agreements?

Concept Files, Volume 2

Indigenous resource management systems
Local institutions for resource management
Collaborative management regimes
Conflicts in conservation
Governance and the rule of law
Decentralizing and devolving government
Common property, communal property and open access regimes.

For further reference

Key question 1.2.9

What specific channels, mechanisms and human resources are available to support participation?

• Are there channels to inform and consult stakeholders about the conservation initiative (e.g., local journals, meeting places, bulletin boards, etc.)? Are they being used for this purpose? Are there specific events (celebrations, rituals, markets) where information can be passed on?

• Are there specific places where stakeholders can interact with the promoters, managers and staff of the conservation initiative and provide advice, discuss activities, and promote or oppose decisions?

• Is there any institution or individual who does or could facilitate a process of negotiation among different stakeholders to achieve a management agreement acceptable by all? Is assistance available to identify and deal with conflicts?

• Could future agreements result in written and signed documents? Could some person or institution provide a secretariat for that?

• Could future agreements be legally binding? On what legal basis? Could someone provide legal counselling to develop an agreement? Would there be a body to settle controversies, should they arise?

• Are there ways by which stakeholders can invest in the conservation initiative (e.g., in terms of money, labour, opportunity costs) with the expectation of future returns?

For further reference

Concept Files, Volume 2

Indigenous resource management systems
Decentralizing and devolving government
Managing conflicts in conservation
Governance and the rule of law
Collaborative management regimes
Cross-cultural communication and local media

What economic resources are available to promote participation?

• Do those funding the initiative recognize the need to involve local stakeholders? Are they earmarking specific funds for that purpose?

• Are the stakeholders themselves contributing or willing to contribute (in cash or kind)?

• What is the likely, and what is the optimum, time period over which funding for stakeholder participation in the initiative could be provided?

Concept Files, Volume 2

Participation: why, what, when, how?
Local institutions for resource management
Indigenous resource management systems
A project or a process?
Economic valuation in conservation
Incentives and disincentives to conservation

For further reference

1.3

Indicators of participation

Indicators	Warning flags
Percentage of local people (or proportion of stakeholders) who know about the conservation initiative, its objectives and management procedures, what to do to contact its management, etc.	Several stakeholders and even key local people (e.g., traditional authorities) are not aware of the initiative
Percentage of people (or proportion of stakeholders) who express confidence in being able to influence the initiative	Stakeholders are very reluctant to talk about the initiative. Answers to questions are yes/no type and the topic is avoided, especially when 'outsiders' are present
Local "ownership" of the initiative (locals talk about it with interest, pride, concern, energy, passion)	Locals talk about the conservation initiative as "your project" or with obvious resentment
	Locals create derogatory names, songs or skits about the initiative
Variety of viewpoints and proposals put forth during meetings where the initiative is discussed	Major meetings to take decisions about the initiative are poorly attended and some key stakeholders are not represented at all
	Meetings are dominated by one person or group pushing sectarian interests
Level of open disagreement expressed in meetings where the initiative is discussed (positive indicator!)	Some stakeholders strongly oppose the initiative, but were never given an opportunity to discuss their concerns with the management of the initiative and/or other stakeholders
Ability of management and staff to list the main stakeholders, their key interests and concerns about the initiative, name a representative for each stakeholder and illustrate the activities carried out to involve them in the initiative	
Ability of stakeholders to represent themselves in discussions about the initiative, to articulate their own interests and concerns and to negotiate agreements with others	Opposition is expressed via acts of rebellion and violence, possibly anonymous (e.g., destruction of information signs associated with the protected area)

Indicators

Warning flags

Most stakeholders lack organization and formal representation

Local leaders (traditional and governmental) are unable to enforce rules and sanctions

Extent to which local leaders support the initiative and attract community support for it

Community protects those who are damaging the initiative (e.g., warning off poachers so they can't be apprehended)

Number and relevance of activities (in the conservation initiative) in which local actors play an active role (e.g., as salaried staff, key advisors, evaluators, etc.)

The initiative is entirely run by non-locals and/or expatriates

Number of local groups and associations that have regular relationships with the initiative

Percentage of local people (proportion of stakeholders) who say they appreciate the conservation initiative and derive benefits from it

The majority of respondents of a given group (e.g., women, or an ethnic minority) state that they receive no benefits whatsoever, or are actually worse off because of the conservation initiative

Average net flow of "investments" in the initiative (per household or per stakeholder, as appropriate)

No local investment (in cash or kind) has ever been made in the conservation initiative

Percentage of local people (or stakeholders) who say they have entered into a relationship or partnership with other local groups because of the initiative

Emergence of new conflicts among stakeholders

Percentage of local people (or stakeholders) willing to enter into collaborative management agreements or take charge of the initiative

Provision of resources and other forms of support for people's participation from local/regional/national government

1.4

Options for action

The following options for action offer some ideas on how local people can be included in a conservation initiative. These need to be considered in the light of specific circumstances to judge whether they are or are not appropriate. You will undoubtedly think of other options as well. The list of options for actions should not be viewed as a step-by-step procedure, although it is set out in the order in which options would be logically considered. (For example, you will need to have identified the stakeholders and informed them about the initiative before you can consider involving them in a planning exercise.) Also, some of the options below are alternatives to one another and need to be compared in terms of appropriateness to the particular context.

The list of options is divided into three groups according to type of activity. These are:

Options to identify stakeholders and inform them about the conservation initiative

1.4.1	Inventory of actual/potential stakeholders
1.4.2	Stakeholder analysis
1.4.3	Information campaign
1.4.4	Public relations service
1.4.5	Environmental discussion sessions

Options to build on the capacities of stakeholders and develop long-term, supportive relationships among them and the conservation initiative

1.4.6	Promoting internal discussion within each stakeholder group
1.4.7	Helping stakeholders organize
1.4.8	Meetings and workshops to build bridges among stakeholders
1.4.9	Visits to similar initiatives with strong participatory components
1.4.10	Strengthening local institutions for resource management
1.4.11	Conservation Councils
1.4.12	Institution for conflict management
1.4.13	Training and incentives for staff and recruitment to fill gaps in skills
1.4.14	Promoting an effective legal basis for participation

Options to involve the stakeholders in the management of the conservation initiative

1.4.15	Assisting local communities to develop their own conservation initiatives
1.4.16	Participatory appraisal and planning
1.4.17	Collaborative management agreement
1.4.18	Collaborative management institutions
1.4.19	Devolving the initiative to local institutions
1.4.20	Participatory monitoring and evaluation

Inventory of actual/potential stakeholders

Option for action 1.4.1

Undertake an inventory of local groups, individuals, institutions, organizations and initiatives with interest and/or involvement in resource management. Take care to include those who use the resources on an erratic or seasonal basis as well as secondary stakeholders (i.e., those who have a 'downstream' interest in the resources, such as users of water flowing from a wetland or purchasers of products acquired from the conservation area). Potential stakeholders (i.e., those likely to acquire an interest as a result of future development of the conservation initiative, such as tourism-related businesses) should also be considered.

A stakeholder inventory is appropriate when the structure of local communities is relatively simple and the stakeholders are easily identifiable. The exercise can be undertaken in a round-table brainstorming session with field staff and the management of the conservation initiative. The inventory will provide an overview of the actual and potential stakeholders and their relative importance and strength. It will also be of great value in indicating the diversity and complexity of the interests which need to be taken into account. In fact, it will provide a basis upon which to identify key partners or groups to participate in the various aspects of the initiative.

After the brainstorming you may want to contact those groups and discuss with them their position regarding the conservation initiative. Consider carefully who is representing the views of the groups, and what biases the positions may reflect. You might want to collect information from more than one member in each group.

Potential obstacles that could be encountered in this exercise are distrust between local people and official agencies, and language and cultural barriers, all of which can hamper the collection of information. Also, inventories need to be updated often to retain their relevance to the initiative.

See Question 1.2.2, Volume 1; and Examples 1a-c in Section 6, Volume 2.

For further reference

Option for action 1.4.2

Stakeholder analysis

Undertake a detailed stakeholder analysis, identifying the relationships of relevant groups and individuals to the area and resources affected by the initiative. Identify local decision-making organizations, the way decisions are made and the holders of relevant specialist knowledge in the community (e.g., resource user groups). Assess the effects the initiative will have on them. Also identify those who could organize activities to discuss and promote participatory prospects in the initiative. Analyze the roles and responsibilities of the various groups and individuals and the ways they could be affected by the initiative.

Specifically include in the study an analysis of the individuals and groups affected by impacts on employment, wealth, nutrition and population dynamics. Consider gender, age, ethnic and class variables. Pay particular attention to any effects the conservation initiative could have on vulnerable groups (e.g., refugees, ethnic minorities).

A stakeholder analysis is more appropriate than an inventory (option 1.4.1) when the communities affected are complex and the stakeholders and their relationships to the resources are not easily identifiable. A stakeholder analysis requires more time and resources than an inventory, since the analysis is usually carried out in the field and involves participatory exercises and the collection of new data.

The use of natural resources is typically characterised by diverse and conflicting interests. For instance, many local communities are socially stratified; knowing the different interests of the various members will help in organizing their participation in the initiative as well as in developing local resource management institutions. Undertaking a stakeholder analysis will also provide a frame of reference for further steps in the initiative and for dealing with various consequences and conflicts which may emerge.

A possible constraint to this exercise is that it requires more expertise in social analysis and community consultation techniques than a stakeholder inventory. Undertaking an analysis can also be costly and time-consuming and, as with inventories, the end product will need to be updated to maintain its relevance to the initiative.

For further reference

See Questions 1.2.2, 1.2.3 and 1.2.4, Volume 1; Information Gathering and Assessment in Section 5, Volume 2 and Examples 2a-c in Section 6, Volume 2.

Information campaign

Option for action 1.4.3

Set up a campaign to inform people about the conservation initiative, its goals, ways of working, its benefits, and the ways in which local people and groups can become involved and benefit from it. If there are prejudices or false information about the initiative, specifically aim to dispel them. Be clear about any potential costs and about what the initiative will and will not do, so as not to create false expectations. Involve local institutions, schools, NGOs, women's groups, community-based organizations, government, and cultural and religious institutions, as appropriate.

Care must be taken to ensure that the forums and methods used do not exclude some sections of the community. For example, some traditional systems may marginalize women and minority groups. Be aware of literacy levels among the stakeholders and adopt suitable communication methods. Use at least some information tools which are not dependent on literacy, such as community meetings, street theatre, or pictorial posters. Household visits may be appropriate where the population is relatively scarce and scattered and literacy levels are low.

As a first step, investigate appropriate ways and means to reach specific user groups. Some may prefer to run their own campaigns with assistance from the initiative. These can interact with the 'official' information dissemination process.

Freely distributed information can help build trust between the management of the initiative and the local stakeholders. A comprehensive information campaign can also greatly increase the level of local awareness, not just about the initiative but about the general state of local resources. Such a campaign will foster a better understanding of the initiative's benefits and costs in both the long and short term. It can also be used to request the stakeholders to identify themselves. If the campaign is used for this purpose it is best to make the request for a display of interest quite general, using simple and comprehensive criteria to define stakeholders.

As a word of caution, problems may arise if information about the conservation initiative is inadequate. Faulty or conflicting information can create a suspicion that the managers are 'hiding something'.

See Questions 1.2.6 and 1.2.9, Volume 1; Social Communication in Section 5, Volume 2 and Examples 3a-f in Section 6, Volume 2.

For further reference

Option for action 1.4.4

Public relations service

If the conservation initiative is large, set up a public relations desk. It should be a place where people can visit to ask questions and offer alternative ideas. It may also be a place to disseminate information, an entry point for relevant databases and, possibly, a coordination centre for consultants and training. Even if the initiative is small, the staff should ensure that local people feel welcome at all times.

Provide an area with an information display about the initiative and show how further information can be requested. Ask local schools, institutions and individuals to visit the display and pose questions. Have a highly-visible suggestion/complaints box (this will work best where people know how to write and are comfortable writing comments). Provide information on the decision-making processes affecting the initiative. If local actors are to influence these processes they need to be aware of how they operate and of the responsibilities of the various agencies involved.

Present information in ways that are appropriate to the area and the initiative. Are the potential users likely to be literate? Consider pamphlets and posters, presentations to schools and churches, guided tours of the conservation area, and audio-visual displays. Recruit local people (artists, teachers, business-people) to design and present the information. Avoid using techniques which give the impression that the initiative has "lots of money" or is top-down and owned by the staff working for it; in some communities, audio-visuals may have this effect. This can lead to unrealistic expectations of what the initiative can provide and undermine efforts to create a dialogue.

It is important that information be made available in the local language, and that it is up-to-date with solid content, to be as useful as possible. A system should be put in place which ensures that all requests for information are dealt with promptly and that people are kept informed of actions taken in response to any suggestions or complaints.

By collecting views and information, the service can also act as a monitoring mechanism, picking up on local perceptions, identifying sensitive issues and stakeholder conflicts as well as positive experiences related to the initiative. It can also be the basis for networking on key issues.

For further reference

See Questions 1.2.6 and 1.2.9, Volume 1; Social Communication in Section 5, Volume 2; and Examples 4a-d in Section 6, Volume 2.

Environmental discussion sessions

Option for action 1.4.5

Organize discussion sessions in local communities, in the local language, emphasising a dialogue approach and using techniques and tools that are culturally appropriate and appealing (e.g., theatre, games, audio-visuals, competitions). Include information on the initiative and its benefits in the local area.

There are many ways to discuss environmental matters that are user-friendly, fun and involve the whole community, including children and the elderly. For instance, helping people to develop a slide show on local problems and resources can be very effective in raising awareness.

The need for conservation should be presented in a non-judgmental way and ideally should arise spontaneously from discussions. People may not be aware of the problems created by their actions or they may be aware of the damage but have few options (e.g., an influx of migrants may have reduced the land available or modern schooling may have meant a loss of traditional knowledge). If people are struggling for survival, they may have no alternative but to rely on the resources in a protected area.

Discussions allow the staff to learn local people's rationale for their actions. Open-ended discussions may improve their understanding of the causes of environmental problems. Staff can then look for solutions that local people feel are beyond their control. Once people have assessed for themselves the importance of conserving natural resources, encourage them to discuss what this implies for their life and work; the costs and benefits of changes; and possible activities to limit costs and optimize benefits. When project staff contemplate a new activity to provide alternative income or replace resources, they would be wise to hold a series of these discussions as a way to sound public opinion.

Hold regular follow-up sessions; one cannot expect a single event to have an impact. Scheduling regular sessions will be appreciated by local people as evidence of staff commitment. Use techniques that are culturally appropriate and financial resources in line with local lifestyles. Also, be prepared to manage possible conflicts (e.g., one group or individual may blame another for the damage to the environment). Lively and meaningful discussion is likely to include differences of opinion.

See Questions 1.2.6 and 1.2.9, Volume 1; Concept File 4.29 (Cross-cultural communication and local media), Volume 2; Social Communication in Section 5, Volume 2; and Examples 5a-f in Section 6, Volume 2.

For further reference

Option for action 1.4.6

Promoting internal discussion within each stakeholder group

Once the stakeholders in the conservation initiative have been identified, contact all of them to request their opinions/advice on various issues and activities, including activities they can undertake themselves. Encourage them to discuss the initiative and the costs and benefits it could bring to the individuals and groups that constitute each separate interest. Each stakeholder group will have a different view depending on their relationship to the resources in question. By first discussing the initiative among themselves, they can clarify their own position before meeting for discussions with other stakeholders. This is a particularly important step to build confidence among less powerful and articulate groups.

Holding discussions within their own interest group encourages stakeholders to clarify their concerns and possibly develop a sense of ownership in the initiative. For the managers of the initiative, the process provides an opportunity to gain insight into the perceptions and interests of local actors and to identify common interests and potential conflicts.

Some stakeholders will not be organized into any sort of group. Bringing them together with others who have common interests can take time and there may be some resistance to discuss matters in an open way when people do not know each other. In such circumstances a facilitator may be needed to call a meeting and make sure that the agenda brings out the common interests of the group. Where there are migratory or erratic resource users, bringing these groups together can be a time-consuming exercise.

The way the meetings are conducted is important. In general, the staff of the conservation initiative should not participate, but should be available to provide any information the stakeholder group may need. It should also be clear that the management of the initiative looks forward to an open and constructive relationship with the organized stakeholders.

For further reference

See Question 1.2.5, Volume 1; Information Gathering and Assessment in Section 5, Volume 2; and Examples 6a-f in Section 6, Volume 2.

Helping stakeholders organize

Where there are power differences that disadvantage some stakeholders, the balance may improve if such stakeholders organize themselves in formal or informal ways. Help such stakeholders to organize (e.g., by offering information, training in managerial and financial skills, access to credit, opportunities to meet with organized groups, opportunities to discuss issues with specific bodies, access to technical, organizational and legal advice, etc.). In particular, non-organized resource users could be assisted to represent themselves in discussions regarding the conservation initiative (travel support, *per diems*, etc.).

Every stakeholder will have different information, concerns and interests which need to be considered and developed. Making sure that all stakeholders are able to develop their own position and form of representation may initially result in more challenges to the initiative. In the longer term, however, through mass mobilization or putting local knowledge to good use, the initiative can greatly increase the level of local support and provide an effective counterbalance to destructive outside forces.

In providing such assistance, it is important that the approach is compatible with the culture and practices of the stakeholders concerned. Whenever appropriate, work within existing social gatherings by adding the conservation issue to existing agendas, rather than holding separate meetings. Avoid setting up new organizations unless there is no alternative. Where some stakeholder groups are particularly vulnerable and have little influence with other stakeholders and decision-makers, you may consider providing support to an umbrella organization, which would group the same interests from a variety of communities (see Example 7a). An umbrella organization may be very effective in attracting funding and expertise to assist stakeholders, and to thus increase their bargaining power.

The duration and scale of the initiative will affect the extent to which stakeholders need to organize (e.g., as informal groups with a common interest or as a formal representative system). It must be remembered that building organizational skills among a disparate group is always a slow process. People need to feel that being part of an organized group is necessary to protect their interests.

See Questions 1.2.3 and 1.2.5, Volume 1; and Examples 7a-d in Section 6, Volume 2.

For further reference

Option for action 1.4.8

Meetings and workshops to build bridges among stakeholders

Organize a series of meetings or workshops with representatives of as many stakeholders as possible, to discuss the need for the initiative and to encourage them to share their views. Start the meeting on a neutral tone, e.g., provide information about the environment and the aims of the conservation initiative. Where there are conflicts among stakeholders, such an approach will help people settle into the subject and feel more comfortable with each other. If necessary, sensitive aspects (such as local causes of environmental damage, or disproportionate benefits) can be dealt with in follow-up meetings.

Be sensitive to when people are ready to come together. They won't cooperate if the meeting is imposed on them. Build on concepts of mutual assistance and common interests. Be aware of power structures within communities and institutions which may inhibit some stakeholders from contributing. Work on avoiding this as much as possible.

If appropriate, invite local authorities, local leaders, etc. to the meetings but make sure their presence does not make people feel uncomfortable when they are expressing their opinions. Pay attention to timing, so that everyone can attend (e.g., women who are busy with household chores). Note who attends and who does not. In planning subsequent meetings, think about how to better contact and attract those who did not attend.

Hold meetings in the local language. Document the discussions and make sure that all participants know when and where they can see copies of these records and copies of any conclusions reached.

The facilitation of these meetings is crucial to their success. If meetings are well-managed, they can provide an opportunity for each stakeholder to hear and appreciate others' views and concerns. This is the basis of constructive interaction among the various interests. If meetings are poorly organized and facilitated, then some stakeholders may not be heard or may be intimidated by others, losing resources and goodwill. When meetings are not successful, positions tend to become entrenched and parties become less, rather than more, trusting of one another.

For further reference

See Question 1.2.4, Volume 1; Concept Files 4.10 (Local knowledge in conservation) and 4.15 (Conflicts in conservation), Volume 2; Participatory Planning in Section 5, Volume 2; and Examples 8a and 8b in Section 6, Volume 2.

Visits to similar initiatives with strong participatory components

Option for action 1.4.9

Organize visits to similar conservation initiatives where local people are successfully and positively involved. Stakeholders can be offered travel support to meet with similar groups and discuss their methods of participation and problem-solving. In preparation for the visit, you may discuss what they should look for, what they can expect to learn and who should go. Follow up with a shared debriefing on lessons learned.

Such visits can be very encouraging for local people, provided the area to be visited has similar problems, a similar culture, and a similar level of resources. The visits provide visible proof that the environment can be improved and that stakeholders can play an important part in the process. Hearing positive information from people like themselves and being able to see concrete results is usually much more convincing than information given by officials or the staff of the initiative. It also provides people with a realistic picture of what is involved in participating, as they talk to people who have been through similar experiences and analyze the problems they encountered and the mistakes they made.

The visits can also assist in building bridges among stakeholders as they share the experience and establish personal relationships. Long-term networks can be established with the people in the demonstration area so that both groups continue to share information and support.

An important point to note is that the area visited must be comparable in terms of natural resources, issues, culture and language. This may not be easy to find in the vicinity. If greater distances are involved, the time and cost involved may decrease the enthusiasm and interest of the local stakeholders and/or funders of the initiative.

There are several issues that need to be considered for this option. Avoid looking only at successes; much can be learned from groups who are experiencing problems. Problems will alert visitors to the potential pitfalls of an initiative. Make sure that a broad range of stakeholders join the group, not just those who are already positive about the conservation initiative. And beware of visiting one area too frequently. Explaining their programme to too many visitors without receiving reciprocal benefits can become a burden to 'model communities'.

See Examples 9a-d in Section 6, Volume 2.

For further reference

Option for action 1.4.10

Strengthening local institutions for resource management

Whether local institutions for resource management (e.g., a forest management committee or a fisherman's group) have a long tradition or are recently established, they can be positively involved in the conservation initiative through specific roles. They can be helped to strengthen themselves by being provided with technology, credit, training (in administrative, managerial and technical skills) or through links with other organizations. But avoid disrupting the local economy, undermining self-reliance or altering social relations, all of which may bring unexpected negative consequences. The initiative should not act in ways which create or worsen disharmony between local interests. For instance, while the power of anti-conservation groups can at times be broken by external interventions, this may not be wise in the long run. They will still be part of the community and may disrupt conservation in many ways. It is better to involve them than to antagonise them.

Enabling local institutions to strengthen their involvement in resource management increases local autonomy, decreases dependency on national and international institutions and funding, and increases prospects for effective local participation in the initiative. Because communities may be stratified, and because there are usually many stakeholders in a conservation initiative, local institutions can become important mechanisms for integrating and mediating between various interests.

In some countries (especially post-colonial ones) local institutions may be weak or nonexistent in significant policy areas, including conservation. It will not be easy to establish new institutions or build up weak ones in such cases. Much time and expert personnel may be needed. It will also take time for any new institution to gain legitimacy. On the other hand, the approach can result in lasting benefits for local communities and the conservation initiative, as local organizations develop the capacity to promote, manage and monitor environmental measures.

The mere existence of local institutions is not enough. They need to be supported by policies and/or legislation which recognizes their right to be involved and to undertake specific tasks (see option 1.4.14).

For further reference

See Questions 1.2.5, 1.2.7 and 1.2.8, Volume 1; Concept Files 4.2 (Indigenous Resource Management Systems) and 4.3 (Local Institutions for Resource Management), Volume 2; and Examples 10a-e in Section 6, Volume 2.

Conservation Councils

Set up a Conservation Council and include representatives of all major stakeholders. A council can provide a key advisory (not decision-making) role and serve as a forum for discussion and consultation among stakeholders. It can identify and discuss resource use, management and tenure; interpret national laws and legislation; draft relevant regulations; identify research needs and needs for infrastructure support, services and policies; and propose specific activities. The council may also be called on to approve/endorse the operating plans of the conservation initiative. But a council, unlike a Collaborative Management Institution (option 1.4.18), is not usually a decision-making body.

Membership in the council will give stakeholders the chance to build skills in procedures policy and negotiating, and will provide an overview of environmental concerns. Members and the groups they represent will likely gain a greater sense of responsibility for the initiative. Over time, if appropriate, the council could provide the basis of a collaborative management institution with decision-making authority.

Because of the council's importance in protecting local interests and disseminating information, members must be representative and accountable, and discussions must not be dominated by a few individuals or groups. All members should have a clear understanding of the council's purpose, roles and powers. They should represent all major stakeholders and both genders. Take care to balance interests; if commercial activities each have a representative, so should each environmental group). Most of all, ensure that less powerful stakeholders with prior rights (e.g., marginalized ethnic groups) do not lose those rights by being subsumed into a group dominated by more powerful players. The council's convenor should be 'neutral' (an NGO or a respected community leader). A chairperson should be elected early on.

Be cautious where there are many stakeholders and diverse interests. The more members there are, the more difficult and expensive it can be to bring them together regularly. The more diverse the interests, the harder it will be to reach agreement. Give thought to paying members who incur expenses or undertake significant responsibilities. Frustration with the system can undermine local support for the initiative.

See Questions 1.2.4, 1.2.7, 1.2.9 and 1.2.10, Volume 1; Concept File 4.16 (Collaborative Management Regimes), Volume 2; and Examples 11a-c in Section 6, Volume 2.

For further reference

Option for action 1.4.12

Institution for conflict management

Ask local people about traditional methods of conflict management (mediation, negotiation, etc.). Build on what exists, identify a relevant new body (e.g., a local council) or nominate an individual to mediate and deal with conflicts between stakeholders and the initiative's management, or among stakeholders. This body or person should be widely respected, and have the trust of all parties involved, particularly indigenous groups. Keep gender issues in mind; both men and women should have confidence in the system adopted. The mediating body must be sensitive to power imbalances between stakeholders (users, regulators, etc.) and be able to maintain a neutral position in the conflict.

Conflict can undermine the viability or sustainability of an initiative. Establishing a formal conflict management system acceptable to all parties prevents conflicts from developing to the point where they are unresolvable and/or violent. Setting up such a system is very complex, however, and should be done only after lengthy public discussion and an exhaustive survey of existing mechanisms (courts, rituals, etc.). Any mechanism established by a short term project is not likely to be sustainable. Staff must ensure that any new mechanism complements existing systems and doesn't compete with them or the authorities that run them (be they local shamans or police). The initiative can really suffer setbacks if the staff don't involve the full range of stakeholders.

There are two main kinds of conflict: conflict among users, and between users and managers/regulators. Each may require a different approach. Conflict among users is often resolved by a commonly accepted mediator. Social and community pressure for compromise can also help. With major power differences it is more difficult; even more so when users and a regulating agency disagree. Often there is a strong sense of mistrust between them, the sides are not equal in strength, community pressure is ineffective and there is political pressure to settle issues quickly and without compromise.

Several factors are particularly important. The conflict management institution must not be seen as being aligned with any party, including management. Those entering into agreements must have the authority to represent their groups. And the conflict management institution must have some power (coercive and/or moral) to enforce agreements.

For further reference

See Questions 1.2.4 and 1.2.9, Volume 1; Concept File 4.15 (Conflicts in Conservation), Volume 2; Conflict Management in Section 5, Volume 2; and Examples 12a-d in Section 6, Volume 2.

Training and incentives for staff to fill gaps in skills

Option for action 1.4.13

Initiate training for the expatriate, local and/or counterpart staff in social communication skills and participatory methods of appraisal, planning, monitoring and evaluation. Emphasize the attitudinal change needed to promote local participation in the initiative and to orient work towards a more "enabling/promoting" role rather than a "controlling/providing" one. You may also consider establishing a system of incentives for the staff of the conservation initiative to reward those who succeed in promoting local participation. This option is not always appropriate, however, and may actually result in 'fake' participation.

It is important to train the staff who actually work with the local people and other stakeholders. Those at management level should also be trained so that they appreciate and endorse the new approach being adopted in the field. This kind of training not only builds skills, it also raises awareness of the abilities and resources of local people and how they can be utilized to make the project more successful. It builds the confidence of field staff in being able to deal with problems with stakeholders so they are more likely to respond in a helpful, constructive way rather than by simply imposing their authority. Training and incentives encourage the staff to become more interested, creative and dedicated to their work.

Training must be relevant to the tasks staff are expected to perform. Most staff members welcome the chance to increase their skills; this in itself is an incentive to better performance. But promises of training that are not kept, or omitting some people from training, can make staff resentful. At best, training should be carried out by people working on similar tasks in similar initiatives who have the capacity to impart knowledge using specific examples. It should be backed up by a period of supervision in the field and by ongoing support until staff are confident with their new roles and skills. A professional may need to be recruited on a temporary basis to perform this role (see case study 13d). At times, it may be necessary to hire a person (e.g., an applied social scientist) specifically to deal with social concerns. He or she would ensure that participatory processes were adopted when identifying and responding to key issues, writing management plans and monitoring and evaluating results.

See Question 3.2.6 and Option 3.4.3, Volume 1; and Examples 13a-d in Section 6, Volume 2.

For further reference

Option for action 1.4.14

Promoting an effective legal basis for participation

Assess the legal basis (legislation, policies and guidelines) for participation of local communities in the conservation initiative. Include an assessment of the status of local institutions for resource management, recognition of communal property regimes, status of local groups (versus governmental agencies with jurisdiction over the body of resources at stake), women's rights to property, etc. Where the legal basis for participation is unclear and/or ineffective, consider hiring a legal councillor to draw a proposal for policy change to submit to the appropriate authorities.

The existence of rights in law is not enough in itself. If the process for claiming those rights is expensive, complicated or slow, the stakeholders, especially the poor, are usually not able to take advantage of them. Such aspects of legislation need to be assessed.

Where changes are needed, more appropriate policies and laws can be promoted via national/regional workshops, national/regional reviews of laws, submissions to the national or local government and political campaigning.

For further reference

See Question 1.2.8, Volume 1; Concept Files 4.3 (Local institutions for resource management) and 4.17 (Governance and the rule of law), Volume 2; and Examples 14a-d in Section 6, Volume 2.

Assisting local communities to develop their own conservation initiatives

Option for action 1.4.15

Through participatory processes, identify which conservation initiatives are already being undertaken or planned in the area, either by the community or by others. Ask local stakeholders which activities they would like agency assistance for, or with which agency operations they would like to be involved. Discuss with them appropriate ways by which this involvement could be achieved.

This option reflects a belief in the value of bottom-up development. Listening to local people and letting them determine the appropriate areas and levels of involvement by outsiders will build self-esteem in the community, and assist in the establishment of constructive interaction between the local community and outside agencies. If the wish for involvement and/or the need for an initiative have come from the community, the commitment to joint planning and management processes is likely to be sustainable.

See Question 1.2.1, Volume 1; Social Communication, and Planning in Section 5, Volume 2; and Examples 15a-f in Section 6, Volume 2.

For further reference

Option for action 1.4.16

Participatory appraisal and planning

Facilitate participatory appraisal exercises (also called participatory action research) by a variety of stakeholders. Deal with the local biological and socio-economic environment, with specific reference to existing interests, capacities and concerns relating to the conservation initiative. Facilitate the development of specific proposals (participatory planning) which can be then submitted to the judgement of the local residents at large (e.g., via referendums, open meetings, etc.) and/or further discussed by the authorities in charge. Ask community groups for suggestions on how they can use their own management systems for the conservation of an area. Compare their suggestions with the ideas of the staff of the conservation initiative. Identify and discuss ways of integrating proposals from different sources. Look out for conflicts and discuss ways of accommodating these.

This process safeguards against technocratic planning being imposed from outside, which too often ignores the interests and capacities of local communities and other stakeholders. Involving affected parties in identifying relevant issues and potential activities can increase their knowledge and appreciation of the initiative and give them a sense of ownership in its future direction. It can also help to reduce the potential for conflict in the implementation stage. In turn, involving the staff and management of the initiative in the exercise gives them a greater understanding of the concerns and capacities of various stakeholders.

Several issues need to be considered before adopting this strategy. First, the process requires the time and involvement of facilitators with experience and training. Such expertise may not be readily available. Also, if the stakeholders do not anticipate substantial benefits, they may be unwilling to commit time and resources to the exercise.

Second, consider the commitment of the decision-makers to take into account the results of the participatory exercise. Failure to do so will create frustration, disappointment and distrust among the participants, which could be very damaging to the initiative. Related to this is the need to ensure that the inputs from the stakeholders are properly recorded, interpreted and utilized so all parties concerned gain the maximum benefit.

For further reference

See Questions 1.2.1. and 1.2.7, Volume 1; Information Gathering and Assessment, and Planning in Section 5, Volume 2; and Examples 16a-h in Section 6, Volume 2.

Collaborative management agreement

Option for action 1.4.17

Support the development of a collaborative management agreement (also referred to as joint management, co-management, participatory management or round-table agreement) in which representatives of all key stakeholders agree on objectives for the conservation initiative and accept specific roles, rights and responsibilities in its management. The process of formulating the agreement should ensure that conflicts are expressed openly, acknowledged, and dealt with.

A collaborative management agreement ensures that the trade-offs and compensations for the stakeholders are clear and that all parties are aware of the commitments made by the other stakeholders. This provides a good structure for internal monitoring and stakeholder accountability. If necessary, identify an external facilitator to assist in mediating and negotiating among stakeholders until a management plan has been agreed upon. Support the plan's implementation and follow-up. Make sure that clear priorities are set for monitoring and evaluation of the agreed activities, and for enforcement and ongoing management of conflicts, as needs arise.

Formulating an agreement among parties with diverse interests requires time, patience and specific skills. Stakeholders will be reluctant to participate if they feel they have nothing to gain by compromising their interests. A collaborative management institution (e.g., a management board, a specific authority, etc.) may need to be established to implement the agreement.

See Questions 1.2.4. and 1.2.9, Volume 1; Concept Files 4.15 (Conflicts in conservation) and 4.16 (Collaborative management regimes), Volume 2; Conflict Management in Section 5, Volume 2; and Examples 17a-f in Section 6, Volume 2.

For further reference

Option for action 1.4.18

Collaborative management institution

Establish a Collaborative Management Institution (e.g., a management board) to develop a management agreement and plan for the territory of the conservation initiative. The institution would also have responsibility for implementing the agreement and the management plan, and for reviewing them, as needs arise. If necessary, the institution could hire a professional facilitator to help negotiate the agreement and plan.

The principal difference between a Conservation Council and a Collaborate Management Institution is that the latter has the power to make decisions. This is essential if the institution is to ensure that the collaborative management agreement is effective. It therefore needs to have some form of legal and/or political status that enables it to enforce its decisions.

The institution would include representatives of all the major stakeholders in the conservation initiative. This would include the governmental agency in charge of management, the local residents in their capacity as users of the resource and/or citizens interested in conservation and/or citizens with unique knowledge and management skills; the local authorities; relevant development and conservation NGOs; and relevant businesses and industries.

As a multi-stakeholder body with an overall knowledge of the initiative and strong local representation, the Collaborative Management Institution provides a most valuable option for the long-term sustainability of the conservation initiative. It may not be easy or inexpensive to set up a new institution, however, even if it can be developed within or alongside an existing one.

For further reference

See Questions 1.2.7, 1.2.8, 1.2.9 and 1.2.10, Volume 1; Concept File 4.16 (Collaborative management regimes), Volume 2; and Examples 18a-e in Section 6, Volume 2.

Devolving the initiative to local institutions

If and when appropriate, and in a way which is compatible with the national political, legal and institutional conditions, devolve the conservation initiative to local institutions. They then become the agents in charge. With necessary initial support, devolution can reduce local dependence on outside assistance, build local confidence and strengthen local management systems, thereby increasing the long-term sustainability of the initiative. And because the people who belong to local institutions live close to the resources concerned and their livelihood typically depends on these resources, they often have an intimate knowledge of the resources and their uses. This knowledge is best tapped if local institutions are given formal authority and security of maintaining authority over time. Devolution can reduce the cost of managing the initiative (at least in the long term) while increasing accountability to the community, since the staff and decision-makers live among those affected by the initiative.

Devolution should not be undertaken until a local institution that can equitably represent local interests and competently carry out conservation tasks has been identified, agreed upon and found willing to take on the relevant responsibilities. The assistance required by the community to undertake the activities expected of them should also have been identified and provided. Such assistance may include training, funding, legislative support and even a degree of ongoing managerial support. Political support for the devolution of authority is essential. Devolution of responsibility will not work if the authority to make decisions is retained at the regional or national level.

A further note of warning: devolving management to the local level can make the initiative more vulnerable to takeover by powerful local or outside interests. This is a particularly serious risk when major businesses and industries are involved.

See Questions 1.2.7 and 1.2.8, Volume 1; Concept File 4.18 (Decentralizing and devolving government), Volume 2; and Examples 19a-d in Section 6, Volume 2.

For further reference

Option for action 1.4.20

Participatory monitoring and evaluation

With the stakeholders, and, if appropriate, the donors, undertake regular participatory monitoring and evaluation to review objectives, approach, activities and results. Monitoring measures progress or compliance; evaluation reflects on the past to make decisions about the future.

Monitoring enables problems to be identified and solutions to be sought at an early stage. It can be carried out on a formal or semi-formal basis by both local people and staff of the initiative. Establish a system to record the results over time; the resulting data can then be part of the evaluation process. Aspects to be monitored could include effectiveness of information systems; regularity of staff visits to communities; maintenance of park boundaries; compliance with meeting schedules, etc.

Stakeholders could be given authority to monitor the quality of service provided by the initiative, e.g., interactions between the local community and management; follow-up to complaints, etc. If stakeholders are responsible for monitoring, there should be a process for feeding results back to management and a commitment on their part to take these results into account. Failure to do so will create frustration and distrust among the stakeholders, which could hurt the initiative. Keep a record of monitoring results, including recommendations to improve the initiative's design, management and scope. Establish procedures and responsibilities for ensuring that decisions are acted on.

Evaluation should reassess the design and objectives of the initiative and assess its impact on the environment and the affected communities. This can be done at planned intervals, when there is a crisis, or if a problem becomes apparent. It should be conducted in open meetings with as many stakeholders as possible. Solicit suggestions for improvement and discuss openly the pros and cons of several courses of action.

Prepare stakeholders for evaluation by providing them beforehand with a list of items. Seek their suggestions on matters to be included. Evaluate not just the initiative but also any changes in the communities since it was implemented. Keep questions broad so as not to confine the analysis. Appropriate questions include: What is getting better? What is getting worse? Who is gaining from the initiative? Who is losing?

For further reference

See Questions 3.2.5 and 3.2.6, Volume 1; Monitoring and Evaluation in Section 5, Volume 2; and Examples 20a-c in Section 6, Volume 2.

Section 2

Addressing local needs in conservation

"Why a reserve here and not elsewhere? What will happen to us? What land shall we cultivate to survive?"

Peasant interviewed on the establishment of the Dimonika Biosphere Reserve, Congo, 1991

2.1

Addressing local needs in conservation

Many years of experience in development and conservation initiatives have shown that conservation and the needs of local people cannot be addressed independently of one another. Development work that neglects the sound management of natural resources is building on shifting sands. Conservation work that attempts to take precedence over the individual and communal concerns of local people is likely to be as successful as the proverbial refrigerator sale in the Arctic.

Combining the two — by pursuing conservation and providing for local needs through the same initiatives and activities — calls for great ingenuity, sociocultural sensitivity, sound economic judgment and sufficient time to develop the optimum solutions that work in unique contexts. Importantly, it also calls for the active participation of the relevant stakeholders. Only local people, in fact, can effectively identify both their needs and the specific compromises that would satisfy them while safeguarding conservation. Only local people can bring to an initiative the wealth of local knowledge and skills they possess.

As a start, the management team could consider local livelihoods in relation to the area's environmental resources. Several of the questions, indicators and options for action in this section will explore this topic and set it within a specific socio-political and cultural context. By fitting into existing livelihood systems, the initiative will stand a much better chance of being owned by local people. At best, however, socially sustainable initiatives go beyond this, and provide new opportunities to generate benefits and economic returns. These, in turn, can help to address local needs and provide incentives to conservation. Non-economic benefits should not be underestimated. They may relate to social status, security of tenure, political autonomy, cultural and religious values, and overall quality of life. In some instances, safeguarding indigenous territories from exploitation by newcomers may be a sufficient incentive for local support.

Two basic approaches have been used by conservation initiatives to respond to the needs and interests of local people:

1. 'De-coupling' the interests of the local residents from the natural resources to be conserved. Thus, projects in buffer zones promote alternative income-generating activities, such as a plantation of fast-growing trees that relieve the pressure on forest timber, cash-crop initiatives, poultry farming, etc. This is meant to shift the economic interests of local people away from the exploitation of resources in a protected area. Similarly, the construction of a road, school or clinic may be offered to the locals as compensation for loss of access to natural resources. Also, better farming practices may be promoted in the lands surrounding a conservation initiative, so that local people are less dependent on its resources for their livelihood. This approach, which often calls for substantial investments from outside, has been the one most commonly adopted.

2. 'Coupling' the interests of the local residents with the conservation objectives. Ecotourism, for instance, brings revenues as long as the local environment is well preserved and worth being visited. Selling game trophies to hunters is viable and lucrative as long as the local habitat is capable of sustaining an abundant wildlife population. Medicinal plants can be collected in the wild and sold as long as they are not over-exploited. And so on. With

this second approach we can also include initiatives such as game-ranching or wildlife-raising projects (such as crocodile, iguana or butterfly farms). Raising a population of a wild and possibly endangered species in captivity may be a positive contribution to maintaining that species in the wild.

Whether a 'coupling' solution is to be preferred to a 'de-coupling' one, or whether a combination of the two is best, can be established only within a specific ecological and socio-economic context. Yet, in all cases we can be sure of one fact: it is not easy to identify ways in which conservation initiatives can produce benefits and economic returns (the 'coupling' approach).

For millennia, rural communities have evolved careful ways of producing from the land while caring for its integrity and thus sustaining production. Today, changes in technology, population dynamics and the widespread shift from subsistence to market-oriented production have strained many of those relationships. For protected areas, in particular, generating economic benefits to be shared among local stakeholders is the exception rather than the rule. Yet, in most situations these benefits must be apparent — locally and non-locally — to obtain support for the conservation initiative. This is the most daunting challenge facing social sustainability in conservation. Some responses to the challenge will be explored in this section of the resource set.

By fitting into existing livelihood systems, the initiative will stand a much better chance of being owned by local people. At best, however, socially sustainable initiatives go beyond this, and provide new opportunities to generate benefits and economic returns.

Such responses can only flourish within a favourable political and economic environment. People have to feel secure in terms of access to resources (security of tenure), and confident of being able to benefit tomorrow from investments made today (political stability). People need to have access to financial means (e.g., credit) and, ideally, to be allowed to use as collateral the natural resources they safeguard with their work. There have to be fair and intelligently-regulated markets, which use incentives and disincentives to assign values to natural resources for their long-term and functional returns, as well as to the health, welfare and culture of people. This section will consider these issues.

This section will also touch on the matter of equity in conservation. Many conservation initiatives involve a range of costs and benefits that are too often unevenly — and inequitably — distributed. Frequently, for instance, local communities with customary rights are forbidden access to resources, and later see such access signed over to commercial companies. Too often, restricted use for pastoralists brings them hardship while agriculturalists gain from an improved water supply from the protected area. Situations such as these are at the root of many failures in conservation.

An effective legislative and regulatory framework would help to prevent inequities by assigning the costs and benefits of conservation in more equitable ways. This could be done by recognizing existing and customary rights; decreasing rather than increasing socio-economic differentiation; and distributing benefits in proportion to both costs sustained and effective inputs of labour, land, capital, etc. A sustainable initiative would carefully regulate this equitable distribution of costs and benefits. Fairness to individuals, not only to user groups or communities, is important to stimulate people to engage in a conservation initiative and to promote long-term investments.

2.2

Key Questions

Key question 2.2.1

How do the natural resources of the conservation initiative contribute to the livelihood of local people?

• How dependent are local people on such natural resources in terms of: food (e.g., by hunting, fishing or using land for agriculture)? Water? Shelter? Fuel? Medicines? Income? Employment? Basic resources in times of emergency? Credit? Other survival needs (as defined by local people)?

• Who actually harvests and uses the natural resources? Are some specific groups more dependent than others on the use of local resources? Which groups (e.g., consider groups of different gender, ethnicity, wealth, education, age, employment status, residence with respect to the boundaries of the conservation initiative)? Are they all dependent on the same resource(s) or on different ones?

• Do the professional team members consider these stakeholders as being different or the same (e.g., women in a community versus men in a community, fishermen versus agriculturists, and so on)? How so? Why?

• Is local livelihood put in jeopardy by the conservation initiative? Are some groups particularly at risk? Are resettlements involved? If so, how does the initiative protect or compensate people? Does the compensation provide for a sustainable livelihood strategy or only for a temporary satisfaction of needs? Does it create a dependence on external resources?

For further reference

Concept Files, Volume 2

Biodiversity and rural livelihood
Local knowledge in conservation
Social actors and stakeholders
Gender concerns in conservation
Population dynamics and conservation
Indigenous peoples and protected areas
Primary environmental care
Social concerns in resettlement programmes

How do the natural resources of the conservation initiative help meet people's cultural, religious and identity needs?

Key question 2.2.2

• How dependent are local people on the natural resources in terms of social customs? Cultural practices? Religious and ceremonial practices? Wealth and status? Security? Privacy? Recreation? Other identity needs (as defined by local people)?

• Are some specific groups more dependent than others? Which groups (e.g., consider groups of different gender, caste, wealth, education, age, employment status)? Are they all dependent on the same resource(s) or on different ones?

• Do the professional team members consider these stakeholders as being different or the same (e.g., people of different religious background)? How so? Why?

• Do sites or species have particular cultural/spiritual significance? Are these protected in the indigenous or customary system of resource management (e.g., sacred groves, ancestral domains)? Do some groups consider themselves owners or custodians of given habitats or resources? Are there specific myths, rites and cultural habits related to the natural resources?

• Is the local culture or social structure significantly affected by the conservation initiative (e.g., by altering resource sharing patterns)? If so, is the management team discussing with people a way of re-planning the initiative or compensating them?

Concept Files, Volume 2

Social actors and stakeholders
Local knowledge in conservation
Applied ethics in conservation
Indigenous resource management systems
Indigenous peoples and protected areas
Local knowledge for conservation
Population dynamics and conservation

For further reference

Key question 2.2.3

Do local people perceive any need to conserve natural resources, specific species, habitats, etc.?

• What are the key problems currently concerning the local people? Is the conservation initiative contributing towards solving these problems? Is it making or will it make any problem worse?

• Do local people perceive any resource/environmental problems? For instance, is there recognized pressure on land or other resources? Is any local resource becoming more scarce (and/or more expensive in local markets)? Are specific species and habitats in danger of disappearing?

• If so, what do local people see as the causes of these problems? Do they see them as being of local or non-local origin? Do they see them as sudden (e.g., a natural disaster) or as structural and ongoing? Do they see them as related to poverty, or related to wealth and power? Do they see them as being at all associated with population dynamics (natural increase or decrease, migration to and from the local area)?

• Do the local people accept that they can/should do something about the problems or do they only see it as a government responsibility?

• Do local people implement/promote/propose/prefer some specific solutions to the resource/environmental problems they perceive?

• Do local people perceive any barriers to solutions? What specifically?

• Is there any local debate on trade-offs between conservation and human needs? Are there any major interest groups? If yes, which ones? Are some in agreement or in open conflict with the conservation initiative?

• Is the local environmental situation perceived differently by different social groups/stakeholders?

For further reference

Concept Files, Volume 2

Biodiversity and rural livelihood
Indigenous resource management systems
Population dynamics and conservation
Poverty, wealth, and environmental degradation
Equity in conservation
Economic valuation in conservation
Local knowledge in conservation
Primary environmental care

Are or were there indigenous or customary resource management systems in the area and are they being affected by the conservation initiative?

Key question 2.2.4

• If yes, what do (did) they regulate? Access to resources? Decisions over access? Resource-use patterns and limits? Seasonal use? Fallow systems? Types of use? Distribution of products? Negotiation of rules and management of conflicts? Other?

• Who is (was) in charge of making important decisions (e.g., resource allocation, labour sharing, conflict management practices)? Are (were) there traditional chiefs, councils of elders, elected councils? Are (were) social sanctions part of traditional management systems? Are (were) there social incentives for sound management and use of resources?

• Are (were) these systems effective? Do (did) they include some specialized knowledge of biodiversity (e.g., relationships between soil types and crop varieties, uses of medicinal plants, inter-cropping patterns)? Do (did) they include zoning to distinguish acceptable land uses? Do (did) they include ecologically-damaging practices?

• Are there evident trends affecting the indigenous or customary resource management systems? What are they? Are they favourable or detrimental for conservation?

• Does the conservation initiative incorporate/support the indigenous and customary systems of resource management (in part or entirely)?

• Are there major differences in resource management knowledge and skills among different stakeholders? How could these affect the conservation initiative?

• Is there a local conservation ethic? Is there a sense of moral obligation to protect the land and other resources for future generations?

• In general, is the conservation initiative consistent with or in contrast to the aspirations of stakeholders and local communities?

Concept Files, Volume 2

Local institutions for resource management
Indigenous resource management systems
Applied ethics in conservation
Indigenous people and protected areas
Biodiversity and rural livelihood
Poverty, wealth and environmental degradation
Local knowledge in conservation
Sustainable use of wildlife

For further reference

Key question 2.2.5

Does the conservation initiative affect access to land or resources and the control over them for one or more stakeholders?

• What is the ownership status of the body of resources at stake in the conservation initiative? Is it state property? Is it under the jurisdiction of a central or local administrative body? Is it subject to more than one form of legal status (e.g., national park and indigenous people's reserve)? Is any part of it private or communal property? If yes, is expropriation foreseen? With what compensation?

• Are there differences of view about who owns the land and resources? Are there any unresolved boundary conflicts or conflicts over rules of access?

• Are there traditional patterns of resource use by local groups that will be restricted or stopped by the conservation initiative? With what compensation? Are alternatives provided?

• Whatever the ownership status, is it respected? Are there problems of encroachment and illegal use of resources? Is tenure secured? Are inheritance patterns clear or controversial?

• Does the country have a system of recognized rights and regulations regarding access to and tenure of resources? Is 'communal property' a recognized ownership regime, or are only state and private property recognized? Are 'indigenous territories' recognized?

• Are there land registries or other records of access rights to resources? Are there specific courts and tribunals where disputes over access and tenure can be discussed and resolved? If conflict over access to resources predated the conservation initiative, how will that be affected?

For further reference

Concept Files, Volume 2

Equity in conservation
Common property, communal property and open access regimes
Indigenous resource management systems
Indigenous peoples and protected areas
Governance and rule of law
Primary environmental care
Biodiversity and rural livelihood

Are there major economic activities (e.g., mining, timber extraction) in the area which do or could affect the conservation initiative?

Key question 2.2.6

• What are these activities? What is their time horizon (short-term exploitation or sustainable exploitation, processing, etc.)? What is the attitude of the people or companies in control of the activities towards the conservation initiative?

• What costs are involved in protecting the conservation area against the negative impact of the economic activities?

• Are the economic activities clearly beneficial to local people and groups? In what ways? How many jobs do they provide (directly and indirectly)? Are there any negative impacts on human health and/or the social environment (e.g., frequent instances of violent behaviour, boom and bust in the local economy)?

• If the activities benefit some stakeholders and affect others (and conservation) in a negative way, are the relevant issues and conflicts well-known and understood? Are they dealt with in an open manner? Who decides on the key matters?

Concept Files, Volume 2

Poverty, wealth and environmental degradation
Economic valuation in conservation
Incentives and disincentives to conservation
Conflicts in conservation
Jobs in conservation
Social actors and stakeholders

For further reference

Key question 2.2.7

Are there incentives or disincentives to conservation in the local context?

• What types of incentives exist to encourage local stakeholders to support and contribute to the conservation initiative? Are there financial incentives (e.g., taxation, matching grants, subsidies, credit schemes, compensation programmes), social incentives (prestige, use of facilities, access to services), or others? Are these incentives known and available to all without discrimination? Can they be enhanced, made more widespread, made better known?

• What types of disincentives prevent local stakeholders from supporting and contributing to the conservation initiative (e.g., are there commercial pressures that prompt people to see conservation as economically damaging; is there any law assigning rights to people who 'opened up' land by cutting down trees and shrubs)? Can the disincentives be minimized or eliminated?

• Can people afford to contribute to conservation? Do they have access to credit, in particular credit that values the management of natural resources in a sustainable way? Do they have access to technical assistance, training or technology inputs when they need them?

• Are political incentives (gaining a share in decision-making power) likely to encourage stakeholders to contribute to the conservation initiative?

For further reference

Concept Files, Volume 2

Incentives and disincentives to conservation
Compensation and substitution programmes
Jobs in conservation
Primary environmental care

What are the actual costs and benefits of the conservation initiative and how are they distributed among the stakeholders?

Key question 2.2.8

• What is the economic value of the resources and products lost to users because of the conservation initiative (loss of access, loss of trade, damage by wildlife, etc.)? What are the other costs suffered by them (e.g., loss of employment opportunities, loss of land, constraints on local business and family income)? Are these felt by all or by some groups in particular?

• What are the economic (and non-economic) benefits accruing to stakeholders because of the conservation initiative (job opportunities, social services, soil protection, clean water, abundance of wildlife, etc.)? Are these distributed to all or to some groups in particular? Do the local people see these benefits as real and/or easily achievable?

• Do local people see these benefits as related to conservation efforts? Do they see them as linked to investments and costs related to the initiative?

• As a whole, who benefits and who loses? Are trade-offs known and clear to all? Have the trade-offs been negotiated and agreed upon in any way? Are alternative opportunities provided to affected stakeholders? Are new social conflicts present/expected as a result of the initiative?

• Is the initiative worsening social inequalities (e.g., making poor people poorer, marginal people more marginalized, women less powerful)? Or is it, on the contrary, attempting to compensate for such inequalities?

Concept Files, Volume 2

Equity in conservation
Gender concerns in conservation
Incentives and disincentives to conservation
Economic valuation in conservation
Social concerns in resettlement programmes
Jobs in conservation
Biodiversity and rural livelihood
Social actors and stakeholders

For further reference

Key question 2.2.9

What contributions can the stakeholders make to the conservation initiative?

• Can the stakeholders offer unique local knowledge and skills for the management of the resources included in the conservation initiative? For instance, do they have their own ways of classifying and qualifying natural resources and habitats? Do local people possess their own ways of monitoring resources?

• Can the stakeholders offer skilled and/or unskilled labour? Can they contribute as a community or as a group, (e.g., by monitoring local biodiversity, surveying for unauthorized access, fire and other hazards)? Can they provide resources and facilities (e.g., for storage, transportation, etc.)?

• Would stakeholders be willing and able to take on the responsibility of providing the conservation initiative with some knowledge, skills, labour or resources, and formalize that responsibility in an agreement with other stakeholders?

• Where outside destructive forces exist, would local stakeholders be willing and able to provide a counter to them (for example by mass mobilization in support of the conservation initiative)?

• To date, has the management team adequately considered/acted on any inputs provided by local stakeholders?

• Can/would stakeholders be able to manage the conservation initiative independently?

For further reference

Concept Files, Volume 2

Local knowledge for conservation
Indigenous resource management systems
Collaborative management regimes
Primary environmental care
Applied ethics in conservation
Local institutions for resource management

Are there solid social and economic opportunities to link conservation objectives with providing for local needs?

Key question 2.2.10

• Is the conservation initiative compatible with the sustainable use of natural resources (e.g., timber and non-timber forest products, fisheries, fodder, agricultural land, wildlife, etc.)? Has the initiative identified/incorporated such sustainable use options? With what results?

• Where conservation objectives and existing resource uses are not compatible, are there viable alternatives to the latter? Are they acceptable to the stakeholders? Can these alternatives help to retain/encourage a stake in conservation?

• Is the conservation initiative compatible with the creation of local job opportunities and income generation activities (e.g., jobs in park management, ecotourism ventures, local business, primary environmental care projects)?

• Will compensation (e.g., economic or via complementary programmes in health, education, adult training, credit schemes) and incentives be likely and sufficient to make the conservation initiative appealing for local stakeholders? Are the links between the incentives and the initiative clear and well-established? Are the economic options provided by the conservation initiative financially attractive compared with the immediate profits from resource exploitation and/or other non-conservation options?

• Are there factors that prevent stakeholders from deriving an income from the sustainable use of resources (e.g., trade restrictions, animal rights legislation, etc.)?

• Are there economic conditions (e.g., international market prices of a locally-produced commodity) affecting local choices that have an environmental impact? Can anything be done to buffer or minimize such external conditions?

Concept Files, Volume 2

Biodiversity and rural livelihood
Primary environmental care
Sustainable use of wildlife
Sustainable farming, forestry and fishing practices
Compensation and substitution programmes
Ecotourism
Jobs in conservation

For further reference

2.3

Indicators of local needs being addressed

Indicators	Warning flags
Percentage of local people (or porportion of stakeholders) who see the conservation initiative as acceptable and/or convenient	People willing to face sanctions and fines to oppose the conservation initiative (e.g., encroachment on protected areas)
	The majority of local people do not see any need for the initiative
	Strong antagonism or distrust among stakeholders (e.g., local people and project or government agents) based on past experience
All indicators of socio-economic and health status, including income per household, literacy, employment rates, morbidity and mortality, etc.	Severe poverty and poor health in some sectors of society while economically valuable resources are protected by the conservation initiative
All of the above in gender-specific, age-specific, ethnic-specific, or class-specific terms (e.g., socio-economic and health status of men versus women, ethnic majority vs ethnic minority, etc.)	
Extent of socio-economic differentiation among local groups	Some local people and groups are benefiting from the conservation initiative, while others are missing out entirely
Local prices of basic foodstuffs and products	
Local prices of natural resources which can be extracted in the conservation area	Endangered wildlife from the conservation initiative can fetch a very high price in local markets
Trends of all the above indicators with respect to the conservation initiative. Are matters improving or getting worse since the establishment of the initiative?	Access to the resources comprised in the conservation initiative is denied to locals but permitted to exploiters with strong economic/ political connections (e.g., the government signed a contract with a commercial company)

Indicators

Changes in local land availability and resource use to accommodate the conservation initiative

Indicators of local population dynamics (migration, fertility, mortality). Trends of such indicators versus availability of land and natural resources and with respect to the initiative

Extent of local knowledge, skills and other contributions incorporated in the conservation initiative

Adjustments of the initiative in response to needs/expectations expressed by locals (e.g., regarding rules of access to resources)

Economic (and non-economic) value of benefits from the conservation initiative directly accruing to local stakeholders

Warning flags

Forced resettlement of people is envisaged/planned/carried out

People migrate out of the area due to reduced access to resources

Increasing population (because of migration and/or natural growth) in the face of stable or decreasing economic options for an acceptable quality of life

Strong contrast between some management practices recommended by the initiative and customary/traditional ones

Land uses in conflict with the conservation initiative are continued and/or intensified

2.4

Options for action

The following options for action offer some ideas on how to provide for local needs in a conservation initiative. They need to be considered in the light of particular circumstances, depending on which they may or may not be appropriate. You will undoubtedly think of other options as well. It is important to remember that the list of options for actions should not be viewed as a step-by-step procedure, although it is subdivided in the order in which options would be logically considered (for instance, you may want to develop a compensation programme only after having completed an assessment of social impact). Also, some of the options below are alternatives to one another and need to be compared in terms of appropriateness to the particular context.

The list of options is subdivided into four groups according to the type of activity. These are:

Understanding local management systems, local claims, needs and potential conservation impacts

2.4.1   Review of indigenous/customary systems of access to resources and resource management
2.4.2   Participatory review of customary claims to land and natural resources
2.4.3   Review of national policies and laws affecting resource management
2.4.4   Assessment of local uses of natural resources
2.4.5   Social impact assessment

Planning to integrate conservation and the meeting of local needs

2.4.6   Open meetings among stakeholders
2.4.7   Special events and 'ideas fairs'
2.4.8   Visits to successful conservation/development initiatives
2.4.9   Building upon local knowledge and skills in resource management
2.4.10   Participatory planning to integrate local needs
2.4.11   Zoning to separate incompatible land uses

Generating benefits for local stakeholders

2.4.12   Primary environmental care (PEC) projects
2.4.13   Jobs for local people
2.4.14   Local distribution of revenues from the conservation initiative
2.4.15   Compensation and substitution programmes

Enhancing the sustainability of benefits to stakeholders

2.4.16   Feasibility studies
2.4.17   Linking benefits with efforts in conservation
2.4.18   Supportive links with relevant services and programmes
2.4.19   Monitoring land tenure and land values in sensitive areas
2.4.20   Incentives to conservation accountability
2.4.21   Biodiversity monitoring and area surveillance by local people
2.4.22   Integrating the conservation initiative with local empowerment in welfare, health and population dynamics

Review of indigenous/customary systems of access to resources and resource management

Option for action 2.4.1

Carry out a comprehensive review of past and present systems of access to resources and resource management. Pay particular attention to uses of resources for local livelihood; established rights of use; local institutions in charge; demarcation of territories occupied and used by indigenous residents; and mechanisms for negotiating agreements and managing conflicts. Involve local people in the review, and discuss with them ways to integrate the effective components of the indigenous/customary systems with the conservation initiative.

The review may provide both a sensible basis for conservation decisions and a set of baseline data for monitoring the benefits and impacts of the initiative. This type of review is best carried out by people who are trusted by and have a mandate to undertake the work from the relevant communities. Indigenous people may be rightly reluctant to release information about some of their customs and traditions to people whom they do not know or trust. The team should also have a sound understanding of the culture, language and traditions of the local communities, to be able to interpret the information provided.

See Questions 2.2.4 and 2.2.5, Volume 1; Concept Files 4.2 (Indigenous resource management systems) and 4.10 (Local knowledge for conservation), Volume 2; and Examples 21a-c in Section 6, Volume 2.

For further reference

Option for action 2.4.2

Participatory review of customary claims to land and natural resources

Organize a participatory mapping session. This exercise can be used to identify land tenure boundaries; areas and resources used by the local people for different purposes; and/or areas where the local people estimate there are environmental problems. (The latter can be focused on afterward to discuss how the problems can be addressed.)

In some cases, the people themselves can draw a map of the intended area and features (see the "Participatory Mapping" tool in Vol. 2). In others, a simple drawing or an aerial photo can be provided by the management of the conservation initiative, to which the people can add as they see fit. Each person present can contribute and identify whatever information is required. It is important that the map contributors include different stakeholders (e.g., women, the elderly, youth, different ethnic and religious groups, land-owners and the landless, business people, local authorities) and that several sessions are held, so that different groups have the time to review and discuss the claims of others.

For further reference

See Questions 2.2.4 and 2.2.5, Volume 1; Information Gathering and Assessment in Section 5, Volume 2; and Examples 22a-c in Section 6, Volume 2.

Review of national policies and laws affecting resource management

Option for action 2.4.3

Carry out a review of national and regional laws and policies affecting national resource management (e.g., laws regulating ownership and access to resources; codes establishing what types of local institutions can have access to credit or enter into partnerships with the government; market regulations, etc.). Assess the stability, compatibility and degree of enforcement of these laws and policies. Involve local stakeholders in the review and, as necessary, in identifying policy changes that would favour both them and the conservation initiative. Make the results of the review available to all stakeholders.

The review will provide key information on the capacity of current policies and laws to integrate local needs with conservation objectives. It will also highlight areas where changes are needed, and whether contradictions exist.

Involving the community in the review process — even if mostly through dissemination of the resulting information — will increase the level of knowledge and awareness among local people of relevant policies and laws, how they are affected by them, and how they can use them.

Too often, policy and legislation concerning natural resource management are both vague and poorly known. On crucial matters, it may be advisable to seek legal interpretation and advice.

See Questions 1.2.7, 1.2.8 and 1.2.9, Volume 1; Concept File 4.17 (Governance and the rule of law), Volume 2; and Examples 23a-d in Section 6, Volume 2.

For further reference

Option for action 2.4.4

Assessment of local uses of natural resources

Prior to setting up the conservation initiative, undertake an assessment of the local uses of natural resources in the area and estimate their ecological impacts. Assess whether the area can absorb these impacts, or whether they are actually or potentially damaging. The assessment should be done in a transparent manner, involving both local users and independent experts. Wherever possible, use research techniques in which local people can actively participate. This will help to build knowledge and awareness about the environment and increase local skills. It will also increase the local community's sense of ownership of the study's findings and recommendations.

The study will help to identify the true causes of environmental damage; the local activities which help to retain/enhance biodiversity; the activities that are compatible with conservation objectives; and the activities that are not compatible and therefore need modifications/ alternatives.

The study described in this option can be technically complicated, especially if several local uses of a resource have combined or contradictory effects. In such cases, singling out the effect of any one such use — and thus assessing its impact — may be quite difficult.

For further reference

See Questions 2.2.1, 2.2.2 and 2.2.3, Volume 1; Concept Files 4.9 (Biodiversity and rural livelihood) and 4.14 (Common property, communal property and open access regimes), Volume 2; and Examples 24a-f in Section 6, Volume 2.

Social impact assessment

Prior to implementing the conservation initiative, undertake a social impact assessment (SIA) involving the various local actors potentially affected. The assessment should provide a basis for integrating the initiative with the resource use practices and values of the local community; build on traditional systems of resource management and decision-making; identify expected costs and benefits and their recipient groups; and design effective information and consultation processes.

Include an analysis of local resource users; local knowledge and practices in relation to resources; scope and capacity of decision-making structures; and local wealth distribution, health status and literacy levels. Specifically include an analysis of the initiative's potential impacts on local health, nutrition and population dynamics. Consider gender/age/ethnic/class matters and vulnerable groups (e.g., refugees).

The assessment should help clarify the initiative's objectives and the means of achieving them. It should also form a strategy for ongoing participation of stakeholders, for developing commitment and capacity at appropriate levels, and for mitigation plans where adverse social impacts are expected. Recommendations should be discussed with the affected groups to ensure that they are appropriate and acceptable. The SIA should include details on implementing and monitoring the recommended measures to reduce the adverse impacts on local groups.

By anticipating the potential effects, measures can be planned to reduce or avoid the negative impacts while creating opportunities to realize the potential benefits. Benefits can take a variety of forms in addition to income-generating activities. Enhanced biomass, improved water supply, recognized and secure access to some wild resources, cultural respect and protection, social rewards and returns for traditional knowledge used by the wider community should all be explored as potential positive effects associated with the conservation initiative.

A possible constraint to undertaking an SIA is that it requires a relatively high degree of skill in social analysis and community consultation; it can also be time-consuming and costly. A potential problem is raising community expectations which cannot be met by making recommendations that are unrealistic (e.g., for political or economic reasons). This problem can be reduced by involving decision-makers in the SIA.

Option for action 2.4.5

See Questions 2.2.1, 2.2.2, 2.2.8 and 2.2.10, Volume 1; Concept File 4.8 (Applied ethics in conservation), Volume 2; Information Gathering and Assessment in Section 5, Volume 2; and Examples 25a-c in Section 6, Volume 2.

For further reference

Option for action 2.4.6

Open meetings among stakeholders

Organize a series of open meetings to identify the expected or current costs and benefits (financial and otherwise) of the conservation initiative. Discuss them and find ways to distribute them as equitably as possible among the various stakeholders. For instance, a meeting could be called to examine in detail a zoning system envisaged by the initiative, as well as the limitations and rules regarding access to resources. Promote the active participation of stakeholders by facilitating, rather than controlling, the meetings. Intervene in discussions only if arguments continue for too long, if some parties dominate the discussion, or when the stakeholders run out of ideas or request further information. If the discussion is going well, let it flow.

This process makes the costs and benefits of the initiative explicit; it identifies potential and existing conflicts and gathers ideas on how they can be resolved through alternative activities. Care must be taken not to raise unrealistic expectations. People will usually place high hopes on the benefits they perceive as 'promised' by the initiative.

Care must also be taken to ensure that the more powerful stakeholders do not dominate the meetings, seeking to protect their interests at the expense of others. Stakeholders who are vulnerable and/or discriminated against may be much less capable or willing to stand up so that their needs are appropriately considered.

For further reference

See Social Communication, and Information Gathering and Assessment in Section 5, Volume 2; and Examples 26a-d in Section 6, Volume 2.

Special events and 'ideas fairs'

Option for action 2.4.7

Organize special events to elicit new ideas for initiatives to link local livelihood with conservation. Establish prizes for the best ideas ('ideas fair') and activities, and link the event with sports matches, market occasions, religious celebrations, etc. to give visibility and spirit to the occasion. Local newspapers and radio stations could promote the event and support conservation awareness. Video shows on conservation issues could be used as a stimulus to generating ideas. Competitions and prizes — not only for ideas but also for concrete achievements (e.g., largest variety of seeds of a given food crop, most efficient irrigation system, largest area reforested by a community) — would link the event with a general promotion of conservation awareness and capacity.

Special events tend to attract a large number of people, especially in isolated areas where gatherings are relatively rare. A special event which incorporates fun, entertainment and competition is likely to receive great visibility. Such an event would provide an opportunity to inform and educate, and to gather and discuss local perspectives and concrete options for action.

See Questions 1.2.9, 2.2.9 and 2.2.10, Volume 1; Concept Files 4.10 (Local knowledge in conservation) and 4.29 (Cross-cultural communication and local media), Volume 2; Social Communication in Section 5, Volume 2; and Examples 27a-e in Section 6, Volume 2.

For further reference

Option for action 2.4.8

Visits to successful conservation/development initiatives

Organize visits for local people to areas with successful examples of conservation initiatives that manage to meet local needs. The visits are not to promote the initiatives but to help people come up with ideas on how they could generate benefits from their own local conservation efforts. It is therefore important to let the people control the discussions and the focus of the visits.

Organize follow-up sessions so that those who took part in the visits can tell others what they have seen and learned. Encourage discussion (possibly with the help of audio-visual aids) about ways to adapt the ideas in practice in the visited community to their own situation. Encourage planning sessions to follow.

Seeing the successes of others is an excellent way to stimulate ideas and action. Discussing the pitfalls that can occur with other communities can also avoid costly and disheartening mistakes. However, care must be taken to avoid people getting carried away with enthusiasm about the success of others and buying into models inappropriate for their particular area.

In addition to stimulating options for generating benefits and meeting their own needs, the visits can also provide the spark to establish local or regional networking groups that pool resources and technical knowledge to solve common problems. These networks, which are geared to field-based experiences, can also get involved in advocacy and providing key inputs for policy-making.

For further reference

See Question 2.2.10, Volume 1; and Examples 28a-e in Section 6, Volume 2.

Building upon local knowledge and skills in resource management

Option for action 2.4.9

Organize retreats, information exchange sessions and development and demonstration programmes to help local people build upon and improve their current management of natural resources. Themes could include enhanced sustainability and efficiency of use, enhanced productivity, more effective marketing, improved control of marketing procedures, product substitution, alternatives to destructive practices, agro-forestry and agro-ecology practices, etc. Value local knowledge and skills, and follow the inclinations and advice of the local people.

This approach increases the local community's sense of confidence in, and willingness to cooperate with, the conservation initiative. It builds upon the pride and self-respect of local people and is effective in mobilizing local support for conservation. Most importantly, it may provide some crucial added skills and capabilities that will result in concrete local benefits.

A problem sometimes encountered with retreats is that they require a considerable investment of time. This can limit the number of staff from the initiative and the local people who can afford to participate.

Care needs to be taken not to follow local advice uncritically — not all local practices are environmentally sound. Where local requests cannot be met by the professional team (e.g., about allocation of budget resources), a proper exchange of views and discussion should be held and decisions should be made in a transparent way.

See Questions 2.2.4 and 2.2.9, Volume 1; Concept Files 4.2 (Indigenous resource management systems), 4.3 (Local institutions for resource management), 4.9 (Biodiversity and rural livelihood) and 4.10 (Local knowledge in conservation), Volume 2; and Examples 29a-e in Section 6, Volume 2.

For further reference

Option for action 2.4.10

Participatory planning to integrate local needs

Carry out a series of participatory planning exercises with various stakeholders, to identify ways by which local livelihood options can be made compatible with and mutually supportive of conservation objectives. Assist by offering facilities for the meetings, facilitation, examples of options, literature, links with groups and institutions that can provide various kinds of support (legal, financial, technical, etc.) and so on.

These exercises are sure to enrich the planning of the conservation initiative by increasing access to local knowledge, information and skills and by ensuring the initiative does not neglect the perspectives and interests of those people most likely to pay the costs of the conservation initiative. In fact, participatory planning provides a powerful mechanism to work out an equitable share of such costs and benefits.

The outcome of these meetings could vary from plans for primary environmental care projects to recommendations for activities and modifications of the conservation initiative to better harmonize it with the requirements of local livelihood.

For further reference

See Questions 1.2.6, 2.2.3, 2.2.8 and 2.2.10, Volume 1; Concept Files 4.19 (Primary environmental care), 4.20 (Sustainable use of wildlife), 4.21 (Sustainable farming, forestry and fishing practices) and 4.22 (Ecotourism), Volume 2; Planning, and Conflict Management in Section 5; Volume 2; and Examples 30a-e in Section 6, Volume 2.

Zoning to separate incompatible land uses

Introduce a zoning system to provide flexibility in the land uses allowed in different parts of the area covered by the conservation initiative. For instance, different zones can define areas where certain species can be hunted or harvested, and other areas where the same species are strictly protected. Involve stakeholders in defining the boundaries of the zones, the uses allowed in each zone and the conditions which will apply to specific uses. Usually, a zoning plan is a crucial component of a Collaborative Management Agreement among different stakeholders.

Combine this exercise with a review of customary resource management systems and resource-use patterns. At best, the new system will reinforce the customary system and minimize the detrimental effects of resource protection on the livelihood of user groups. Stakeholders can be granted different rights at different times even within the same zoning system. For instance, indigenous peoples may be granted special access to some resources in recognition of their customary rights and sound use practices.

See Options 2.4.1, 2.4.4, 2.4.10 and 1.4.17, Volume 1; Concept Files 4.2 (Indigenous resource management systems) and 4.16 (Collaborative management regimes), Volume 2; Planning in Section 5, Volume 2; and Examples 31a-d in Section 6, Volume 2.

For further reference

Option for action 2.4.12

Primary environmental care (PEC) projects

Help local people develop their own primary environmental care (PEC) projects. PEC projects combine local environmental care with meeting local needs. The projects would be run by local organized groups and could be assisted by or linked with the conservation initiative in several ways. For instance, some staff of the conservation initiative can act as 'matchmakers' to assist local groups in obtaining the inputs which they themselves identify as being crucial for projects to succeed. Such inputs may include credit, specific technologies, political support, training courses, networking with similar projects or study visits, as well as specific information and advice.

In some cases a rotating fund can be established to support the best community-generated projects that meet PEC criteria. This is particularly appropriate when capital is available (e.g., through a trust fund) to support both environmental conservation and people's welfare.

PEC projects build local confidence and strengthen the capacity and skills of local organizations. When they are closely associated with the conservation initiative, they effectively enhance the local support and thus the sustainability of the initiative itself.

For further reference

See Questions 1.2.5, 2.2.3 and 2.2.10 and Options 1.4.15 and 2.4.10, Volume 1; Concept File 4.19 (Primary environmental care), Volume 2; and Examples 32a-f in Section 6, Volume 2.

Jobs for local people

Option for action 2.4.13

Provide jobs within the conservation initiative for local people, especially for those disadvantaged by it. If necessary, establish training programmes for people to acquire the necessary knowledge and skills. If not enough jobs are available in the conservation initiative, explore whether they can be provided elsewhere, and facilitate the hiring of local residents (e.g., by assisting them in obtaining information, transportation, training, etc.). It may also be possible to create new jobs, such as recycling waste or producing materials locally rather than importing them.

As well as providing a means to replace income lost through restrictions imposed by the initiative, creating jobs for local people can be good for the long-term sustainability and work-force stability of the initiative. Local people are usually more committed than outsiders to staying in the area. Also, employment in work which is dependent on the success of the initiative increases the sense of ownership of and commitment to the initiative within the local community. Employing local people can also increase local control of the initiative and promote the use of local knowledge.

In areas where there is a shortage of employment opportunities, there may be intense lobbying and competition for jobs among various local groups. If not carefully handled, this may damage the relationship between the initiative and the local communities. Managers should avoid employing relatives and friends. Salaries should be compatible with local pay scales to avoid creating major economic disparities in the community and thus promoting envy and conflict.

Jobs established on the expectation they will be permanent (because they are replacing other sources of income lost as a result of the initiative) should be financially solid. Failure to sustain such jobs could leave the local people worse off than they were before, and result in ill feeling towards the initiative. Economic feasibility studies of any job-creation projects should be undertaken before they are implemented and it should be clear from the outset which jobs are expected to be only temporary and/or seasonal.

See Questions 2.2.1, 2.2.6, 2.2.9, 2.2.10 and Option 2.4.16, Volume 1; Concept Files 4.19 (Primary environmental care), 4.22 (Ecotourism) and 4.24 (Jobs in conservation), Volume 2; and Examples 33a-d in Section 6, Volume 2.

For further reference

Option for action 2.4.14

Local distribution of revenues from the conservation initiative

If the conservation initiative is capable of generating an income flow (e.g., via ecotourism or culling of wildlife), then identify, together with the interested parties, a way to distribute a part of such revenues locally. The distribution could be carried out in different ways. Revenues could be shared equally among all the households in a village; they could be shared proportionally to needs, or to damages suffered because of the conservation initiative; or they could be used to build a local "livelihood fund". The fund would finance local projects, in particular, projects to benefit the social groups disadvantaged by the initiative. Whichever system is used must be transparent and accountable and agreed to by all the stakeholders.

An advantage of this approach is that it directly links specific benefits with the existence of the conservation initiative. The option should, however, be approached realistically. Very few conservation initiatives have the potential to generate large sums of money. Where revenues are small, they may not be a sufficient incentive for people to participate (i.e., to spend time and resources) in developing communal initiatives. It also may not be feasible to share them equally among households. In such a situation, investing the revenues for some community development project may be an interesting option, especially if the project can serve the interests of local people in an equitable way. Alternatively, when revenues are substantial, it may be difficult to convince government authorities that the local people are entitled to a sizeable share.

The management of the revenues should be carried out in a competent and transparent way, following established rules. A written record of how the funds are distributed should be kept, and made available to the public.

For further reference

See Questions 2.2.7, 2.2.8 and 2.2.10, Volume 1; Concept Files 4.23 (Compensation and substitution programmes), 4.25 (Economic valuation in conservation) and 4.26 (Incentives and disincentives to conservation), Volume 2; Planning in Section 5, Volume 2; and Examples 34a-f in Section 6, Volume 2.

Compensation and substitution programmes

Carry out an economic evaluation of the resources to which some people will lose access, or which could suffer damage as a result of the conservation initiative (e.g., serious damage to crops and livestock can be caused by wild animals protected by the initiative). Carry out an assessment of potential compensation and substitution programmes (e.g., rotating funds for local development projects, systems to compensate for actual damage, systems to replace a protected resource with another local or non-local product). If the programmes are deemed feasible and effective, implement them. The programmes should aim at increasing self-reliance, compensating for damages and maintaining quality of life, but should strive to not create a dependency on outside resources.

Compensating for losses experienced by individuals or a community as a result of a conservation initiative reinforces the initiative itself. Unfortunately, the mechanisms to provide monetary compensation to individuals who have suffered specific losses (e.g., crop damage by wild animals) can be cumbersome and difficult to keep transparent and honest.

Substitution programmes can also provide a means of compensation. Often, however, local people whose livelihoods or basic needs are dependent on the resources to be protected will stop using those resources only if and when an alternative is provided.

Initiating and establishing compensation and substitution programmes can consume both time and energy and are demanding in terms of staff time and skills. Ingenuity, social sensitivity and economic skills are needed to design adequate provisions to balance major changes in lifestyle and production systems consequent to a conservation initiative.

See Questions 2.2.1, 2.2.2, 2.2.7, 2.2.8 and 2.2.10, Volume 1; Concept Files 4.23 (Compensation and substitution programmes) and 4.26 (Incentives and disincentives to conservation), Volume 2; and Examples 35a-e in Section 6, Volume 2.

For further reference

Option for action 2.4.16

Financial feasibility studies

Carry out studies of the practicality and economic viability of the activities that have been proposed to provide for local needs within the conservation initiative. Undertake thorough market research on the demand for products, the likely income and the establishment costs. Organize meetings to discuss and expand on the results of the studies with all potentially affected groups. Make sure that the people who start commercial activities associated with the conservation initiative are supported by appropriate business training. Financial feasibility studies backed up by appropriate training will ensure that all concerned have realistic expectations.

Feasibility studies generally require a variety of skills and knowledge. Depending on the venture to be examined, these may include market and consumer analysis, business management, accounting, processing, etc. Involving local people who have knowledge relevant to the proposed production and tapping into voluntary expertise in the wider region may lessen the need for expensive professional advice. Nevertheless, relevant expertise is often needed; the conservation initiative may find it appropriate to offer this type of support. The cost of failure for both the local people and the initiative may be too high to warrant unnecessary risks.

For further reference

See Question 2.2.10 and Options 2.4.12, 2.4.13, 2.4.14 and 2.4.15, Volume 1; Concept Files 4.19 (Primary environmental care) and 4.25 (Economic valuation in conservation), Volume 2; Information Gathering and Assessment in Section 5, Volume 2; and Examples 36a-c in Section 6, Volume 2.

Linking benefits with efforts in conservation

Option for action 2.4.17

Identify mechanisms that proportionally reward the efforts of individuals or groups in the conservation initiative. Efforts include all contributions: labour, land, equipment, expertise, as well as costs borne, etc. The mechanisms could be ongoing (such as assurance of tenure, or payments for conservation tasks on the basis of the obtained conservation results), or time-specific (such as a prize or reward for particular achievements). Explore culturally relevant mechanisms of rewarding merit (e.g., ceremonies and public recognition may be part of the benefit expected and desired). Consider linking benefits with zoning arrangements.

This approach reinforces the message that the contribution of local stakeholders to the initiative is important, noticed and valued. It also creates a built-in positive reinforcement of good practices.

There are, however, two potential problems that need to be considered before proceeding with this option. First, the contributions people make towards the initiative need to be seen in proportion to what they are able to give. For instance, while wealthy people may contribute a great deal of money, this may only be a small sacrifice for them. A mother who offers some of her time after working in the fields and looking after a house and family contributes much more in relative terms.

The second potential problem is identifying who contributes what. This is especially difficult in cultures where people work mostly in groups. In such cases it may be more appropriate to reward a group or an entire community rather than individuals.

See Question 2.2.9 and Options 2.4.11, 2.4.12, 2.4.13, 2.4.14, and 2.4.15, Volume 1; Concept Files 4.19 (Primary environmental care) and 4.23 (Compensation and substitution programmes), Volume 2; and Examples 37a-c in Section 6, Volume 2.

For further reference

Option for action 2.4.18

Supportive links with relevant services and programmes

Identify and pursue potential supportive links between the conservation initiative and programmes of various governmental sectors (e.g., health, education, agriculture, etc.) as well as NGO- and community-based programmes operating in the area. For instance, link participatory planning exercises for the management of natural resources to participatory planning for primary health care, to projects promoting women's and children's education and training, and to agro-forestry training schemes, rural credit schemes, family planning services, etc.

The first purpose of forming these links is improving local livelihood by all available means and methods; conservation of natural resources cannot be sustained in the face of deteriorating living conditions. The second purpose is to gain maximum benefits from the services and resources available. Links will also ensure that other programmes and services operating in the region are aware of the initiative and its objectives.

The benefits of linking may be as direct and simple as sharing facilities and means of transportation. They may also be major and forward-looking, such as the conservation benefits of stabilizing local populations when appropriate health and family planning services are widely available.

The crucial importance of this option should not be underestimated. There is little logic in trying to provide local people with incentives to conservation when their most important concerns (health, education, the local economy) are being neglected.

For further reference

See Option 2.4.12, Volume 1; Concept Files 4.4 (Population dynamics and conservation) and 4.26 (Incentives and disincentives to conservation), Volume 2; and Examples 38a-f in Section 6, Volume 2.

Monitoring land tenure and land values in sensitive areas

Option for action 2.4.19

Establish a system to monitor land ownership and land values in sensitive areas, such as buffer zones around protected areas. In territories undergoing rapid land–use changes, such as agricultural frontier regions, land markets can be volatile and unpredictable. Speculative forces often operate a step ahead of legislation, and can undermine efforts at establishing protected areas, special management zones, and community-based conservation. This is particularly important when indigenous peoples are involved. Ongoing monitoring can provide the conservation initiative with key information about the forces at work in and around the natural resources at stake.

The principal aims of the monitoring system would be to establish a baseline situation and ground rules in terms of access to and tenure of natural resources. The system would be useful for highlighting existing contradictions and conflicts when trying to reach mutually agreeable solutions. Once solutions are found, the monitoring would help detect violations of agreements.

The monitoring system can be run either by a local committee comprised of key figures of the region or community, or by an independent technical entity. If available, a geographic information system (GIS) or computer-based mapping technology may be used to store and analyze information. The system may combine a review of public registries with extensive field work, including workshops and participatory surveys. It should be noted that a land tenure monitoring system can be relatively expensive and time-consuming and is usually applied on a limited scale, specifically in very sensitive areas for conservation, or in areas of rapid land-use change.

See Options 2.4.2 and 2.4.3, Volume 1; Monitoring and Evaluation in Section 5, Volume 2; and Example 39a in Section 6, Volume 2.

For further reference

Option for action 2.4.20

Incentives to conservation accountability

A number of mechanisms can be devised and established to link a benefit or return to appropriate management practices. For instance, tenure of a given piece of land and permission to use a certain resource can be made conditional on the quality of resources on that land or on the quality of the management of the resources. Obviously, reference standards and guidelines should be well known to all the parties.

Care needs to be taken in adopting this option. In general, it works best when the wish to manage resources in a sustainable way is internalized (i.e., accepted wholeheartedly) by the users of resources. Incentives which rely on project funds should be avoided.

For further reference

See Questions 2.2.7 and 2.2.9, Volume 1; Concept File 4.26 (Incentives and disincentives to conservation), Volume 2; and Examples 40a-d in Section 6, Volume 2.

Biodiversity monitoring and area surveillance by local people

Option for action 2.4.21

Discuss with local people whether they wish to take on the task of monitoring local biodiversity in the territory covered by the initiative. If they do, agree on procedures and responsibilities to ensure that, when problems are identified, they are acted on quickly.

Monitoring biodiversity is one of the most interesting contributions that local people can provide to a conservation initiative. Usually they have both an interest and a comparative advantage in doing the work, because of their easy and frequent access to resources, and because of their detailed knowledge of places and local ecology. Many local residents, for instance, recognize signs of change that are not obvious to non-local observers.

Indicators for the monitoring exercises would be agreed to by the local people and the initiative's staff, as would the reporting schedule and any compensation. In some cases, maintaining local biodiversity would be sufficient reward; in others (especially in very poor communities), explicit compensation may be needed; this can take a variety of forms. In some cases, a community may be assured of access to harvesting a given quantity of resources in exchange for monitoring biodiversity. In others, an economic return may be given (for the whole community or for a salaried individual). In general, it would be advisable to include this option in a general discussion of roles, rights and responsibilities of stakeholders regarding the conservation initiative (see option 1.4.17).

Local people can also effectively carry out surveillance of an area or set of resources. For instance, they can watch for outsiders who try to exploit resources in illegal ways (see example 41d). Surveillance may also refer to phenomena such as fire, floods and landslides. Local residents do have a comparative advantage (and often a direct interest) in recognizing risk factors and early warnings of disastrous events such as fire and floods. If properly supported by relevant social services they can carry out valuable and effective work in disaster prevention.

In surveillance work, local residents should not try to apprehend the violators (which in most countries would be illegal), but instead communicate quickly (e.g., by radio) with the relevant authorities. Specific rewards may be agreed upon as an incentive.

See Question 2.2.9, Volume 1; Concept Files 4.20 (Sustainable use of wildlife), 4.21 (Sustainable farming, forestry and fishing practices) and 4.22 (Ecotourism), Volume 2; and Examples 41a-d in Section 6, Volume 2.

For further reference

Option for action 2.4.22

Integrating the conservation initiative with local empowerment in welfare, health and population dynamics

Promote participatory assessment and planning exercises in which initiatives in natural resource management and local welfare and population dynamics are dealt with in an integrated fashion. Lobby authorities to enhance local capabilities for income generation, job training, basic education (especially for women), reproductive health and family planning, and to facilitate a good measure of local awareness and control of local migration phenomena.

Poverty, disease and rapid changes in local population (growth and decline) have a powerful affect on the management of resources. If the conservation initiative is not concerned with local welfare, health and population dynamics, it may become incapable of dealing with phenomena such as deteriorating quality of life and inequitable distribution of resources. These are often at the root of the opposition and conflicts that undermine the sustainability of conservation initiatives.

This option does not at all imply that the initiative become directly involved with providing family planning services, health care or income-generating opportunities. It does, however, suggest that the initiative help local stakeholders (including government authorities) to consider and discuss resource management issues together with issues of local welfare and population dynamics. Once the relevant actors (e.g., government agencies or NGOs working with local people) have decided what they wish to do about these issues, the initiative may support them (in direct or indirect ways) to take appropriate action.

For further reference

See Questions 2.2.1, 2.2.2 and 2.2.3, Volume 1; Concept Files 4.4 (Population dynamics and conservation) and 4.19 (Primary environmental care), Volume 2; Information Gathering and Assessment, and Planning in Section 5, Volume 2; and Examples 42a-b in Section 6, Volume 2.

Section 3
Managing a sustainable initiative

"… I have worked with lots of people from the North and I am sick of it. They got all my support in the field but I have never seen my name in their papers. When we carry out a project together, they are paid ten times my wage, and get all the fringe benefits…"

Latin American anthropologist, Peru, 1987

3.1

Managing a sustainable initiative

This section considers how an initiative can deal with its most immediate social concerns: those of the people who work for it. Most conservation initiatives involve the long-term management of territories and the natural resources they contain. This is the "environmental management" we have so far discussed in this volume; have argued could be carried out in a participatory manner (Section 1); and could meet conservation objectives while providing for local needs (Section 2). The initiative itself, however, needs to be managed and remain viable in the long run, and the way in which this is sought after is a determinant of social sustainability in its own right.

The skills, attitudes and commitment of the team in charge of the initiative; the quality of the relationships among them and with stakeholders and the community at large; the openness and fairness with which the team deals with conflicts and change; the reconciliation of personal and professional goals — all of these factors have an impact on the initial success and long-term sustainability of the initiative. Using the term "internal management" in regard to such an initiative thus means the structure, practices, attitudes and work styles of the people working for it.

In the case of a protected area, "internal management" would refer to the ways in which the local branch of the government agency responsible organizes its work; shares tasks and responsibilities; hires, motivates and rewards staff; facilitates internal communication among staff and external communication with local stakeholders; evaluates its own work; and so on. In the case of a project (e.g., a three-year support of the rehabilitation of a watershed), or a programme (e.g., the development of institutional structures and long-term management of a coastal area) "internal management" would refer to the management style of the team in charge. The details may differ from one case to the next, but the principles for social sustainability are similar.

Why is internal management important? Promoting the participation of local stakeholders without practising participation within the initiative is at best contradictory and at worst hypocritical and ineffective. Management studies show how important the structure of an organization is for the success of its goals — no matter what they are. For instance, organizations that are 'flat' (non-hierarchical), friendly and supportive of personal initiative and team spirit are more capable of responding to demanding and complex tasks. Such organizations seem to be able to make optimal use of the capacities of the staff and productively channel the energy too often wasted in internal struggles, resentments and bureaucratic red tape. No one model, however (not even non-hierarchical and participatory management), is good for all occasions. Every initiative needs to develop its own approach, although awareness of various approaches is invariably useful.

A few other points of general validity. First, the quality and commitment of the initiative's staff is paramount for its success both in terms of conservation achievements and communication with stakeholders. Investing in the staff usually pays off. Second, the time horizon to assess consequences and impact should be fairly long (several years or so). Complex integration of biological and social resources does not happen from one day to the next. Third, staff drawn from the community, community volunteers, co-opted or elected community members of working groups, etc. are also part of the conservation initiative. These people are perhaps the most vulnerable to exploitation. Too many tasks, too little supervision, insufficient support and encouragement, poor communication — all of these may contribute to such people feeling undervalued and left out, especially when they may be the ones working in the heat and dust. They may also be the least educated, and yet their need for training is not often recognized, even though the long-term sustainability of the initiative depends upon their skills and enthusiasm.

This section takes a professional team working for conservation through some key questions, indicators, warning flags and options for action to reflect upon and evaluate their own work style and effectiveness. This can be a difficult and at times uncomfortable process. If serious conflicts surface, it may be useful to bring in an independent facilitator to guide the process in a constructive manner.

The skills, attitudes and commitment of the team in charge of the initiative; the quality of the relationships among themselves, with stakeholders and with the community at large; the openness and fairness with which the team deals with conflicts and change; the reconciliation of personal and professional goals — all have an impact on the initial success and long-term sustainability of the initiative.

3.2

Key Questions

Key question 3.2.1

Is the initiative run as a project or a process?

• Is the initiative run as a project (set approach, objectives, time limit) or a process (ongoing and adaptable in response to lessons learned)?

• What is the time horizon of the initiative? Is there a balance among long-term, medium-term and short-term objectives and activities? Are work schedules and phases realistic?

• Who identifies the initiative's specific objectives, activities and deadlines? Is it the local staff of the initiative? Local staff and various stakeholders? People not involved in running day-to-day activities?

• Is there enough flexibility in carrying out activities that opportunities and constraints can be met as they arise and not ignored because of prior planning?

• Are monitoring, evaluating and reviewing/replanning activities carried out on an ongoing basis? Are mistakes acknowledged and learned from, or do they go unrecognized and unacknowledged?

For further reference

Concept Files, Volume 2

A project or a process?
Management styles

What is the initiative's management style?

• Is the initiative run on a strict hierarchical basis? Are individual ideas and endeavours rewarded or repressed? Are decisions imposed or discussed? Are the bases of decisions generally known by the staff or not known? Is there openness to new ideas and ways of working?

• Are all the decision-makers in the initiative accountable to someone directly supervising them? Are they also accountable to staff at large? How is accountability established and ensured?

• Is the initiative as a whole accountable to stakeholders?

• Are staff treated in a respectful and friendly way, or are they harassed and kept in fear and insecurity? Do managers tend to hide information from staff and lie to them? Do staff tend to hide information from managers and lie to them?

• Are internal bureaucratic requirements reasonable or cumbersome? Can necessary changes be made quickly? How many people are involved in making a decision of medium importance?

• Is the initiative's budget open to scrutiny? Are purchasing policies transparent to all? Do staff discuss budget decisions with managers?

Concept Files, Volume 2

Management styles

For further reference

Key question 3.2.3

How are the staff managed and motivated?

• How are the staff recruited? Is recruitment decided by one person or by a team? Is there a bias in terms of gender, ethnicity, religion, caste or other characteristic? Why is this so? Does this have consequences for the conservation initiative?

• Are the local groups most affected by the initiative represented in the composition of the staff? Are local people given employment preference over expatriates of equal ability? Is knowledge of the local culture and systems valued and reflected in the recruitment of professional staff?

• How is staff morale? On what basis are staff evaluated and rewarded? Are they confident about job tenure? Are there clear (and flexible) job descriptions? Are there opportunities for professional development and capacity-building? Are staff overworked? Are staff often idle?

• Will salaries maintain families in decent living conditions? What is the gap between the top and bottom salaries of the technical staff? Are there differences in the salaries of technical staff among disciplines (e.g., biologists and social scientists)? What is the salary and benefits gap between local and expatriate staff and between national and local staff? Are the gaps justified and accepted by everyone?

• What is the gap between technical staff members in terms of use of vehicles, secretarial support, use of budget resources for travel, *per diems*, etc.? Are these gaps justified and acceptable to everyone?

• For staff working in the field, is adequate provision made to compensate or redress any lack of essential facilities in the area concerned?

• Where personal risk is involved, are staff provided with adequate protection or security back-up? Are staff provided with adequate equipment/facilities to carry out their responsibilities?

• Is there a staff association, union or some other organization to represent staff interests? If the need arises (e.g., attacks from vested interests), are staff and management willing and able to support each other?

For further reference

Concept Files, Volume 2

Local knowledge for conservation
Indigenous people and protected areas
Management styles

What is the quality of internal communication among the staff?

Key question 3.2.4

• Is information shared among the staff or is it kept and used by individuals? Are there regular staff meetings, bulletin boards and other means by which staff members can inform one another about their work, problems and opportunities?

• Is team work promoted or avoided? Do all staff participate in assessing problems and opportunities, and in planning, monitoring and evaluating activities?

• Are staff usually open and vocal in disagreements, and in suggesting alternative courses of action? Are such suggestions sought and welcomed by the managers in charge?

• Are there groupings and alliances among staff, with some in opposition to others? Are instances of open conflict among staff frequent or rare? Are there accepted ways of mediating conflicts? Who makes the final decision in the case of persistent disagreements?

• Are managers credible in the eyes of the staff? Are staff professionally valued by the managers?

• Are there opportunities for exchanges of ideas and experiences between staff working in different projects or between different sections of the initiative?

Concept Files, Volume 2

Management styles

For further reference

Key question 3.2.5

What is the quality of communication between the staff of the conservation initiative and the local stakeholders?

• Do the staff of the initiative speak the local language and interact with local people in social terms? Are there social events in which both staff and local people participate? Do staff show respect for local customs and values? Do local communities appear to value the professional and personal qualities of the staff of the initiative?

• Do staff tend to generalize the characteristics of local people or of certain groups of local people (e.g., "they are all too clever", "they are lazy", "they are poachers", etc.)? Do local people do the same about the staff (e.g., "they care only for animals", "they are corrupt", "they cannot be trusted", etc.)?

• Are the managers and staff of the initiative credible in the eyes of local people? Do they have something to offer that is valuable in the eyes of the locals? Is their expertise generally recognized?

• Are local people entirely dependent for information on what the staff of the conservation initiative pass on to them, or have they some means of requesting information? Do local people often initiate relationships, e.g., by asking for support, advice or by demanding some change in the practices of the initiative? If yes, is the staff accessible? Are requests handled promptly and fairly?

• Is there a way for stakeholders to transmit complaints regarding their relationship with the staff of the conservation initiative?

For further reference

Concept Files, Volume 2

Cross-cultural communication and local media
Local knowledge in conservation
Management styles

Are the staff's capacities and work plan suited to the initiative?

Key question 3.2.6

• When hiring technical staff, how is practical and local experience valued compared to academic background or international experience?

• Is an appropriate variety of capacities represented among the staff (e.g., physical and social sciences, local work experience, local languages, etc.)? Is capacity appropriately matched to roles and tasks? Is the gender, age and level of education or ethnic background of the staff appropriate to ensure effective relations with various stakeholders?

• Do any/many of the staff have special training in social issues in conservation?

• Do the staff work in a multi-disciplinary way or is the organization a collection of different professionals working in isolation? Are social issues placed in a separate department, isolated from mainstream work?

• Is the monitoring and evaluation function cut off from day-to-day work or is it integrated into ongoing activities?

• Is most staff time spent in the office on administrative tasks, or in the field? Is the main office close to the field or in a 'convenient' town?

• Is the work schedule attuned to the timing of activities in the local communities (e.g., major planning meetings scheduled for less busy times of the year)?

• Are the managers and staff exposed to current literature and debates on conservation?

• Is any ongoing research element incorporated in the work plan? Are the results of such research (and/or the lessons learned in everyday work) incorporated in the initiative's work plan?

• Ultimately, is the staff committed to the work? Do they believe they are achieving the results they had in mind?

Concept Files, Volume 2

Management styles

For further reference

3.3

Indicators of sustainable internal management

Indicators

Percentage of deadlines met, results achieved on time

Instances in which the work plan has been substantially modified as a positive response to lessons learned along the way

Efficiency with which staff are able to deal with management challenges/emergencies

Percentage of staff satisfied with employment conditions, and feeling professionally rewarded

Percentage of staff appreciative of the professional qualities of colleagues, and in good communication with them

Variety of social characteristics, background and capacities represented among the staff

Frequency, openness and effectiveness of staff meetings, and meetings to plan/evaluate ongoing work

Adequacy of lowest staff income/ benefits to provide a decent living to an average family

Frequency and quality of interaction (both professional and social) between staff, local people and stakeholders

Warning flags

Time horizon of the initiative clearly unrealistic to achieve expected results, frequent delays

Frequent confusion of staff regarding meetings, appointments, schedules

Staff morale exceedingly low, frequent verbal fights, lack of cooperation

Disagreements about the goals of the initiative among staff

Only men, only expatriates, only biological scientists in senior managerial positions

Some staff have incomes and benefits clearly insufficient to maintain a family

Staff say that they "have no time to deal with local people", they "have no time to go to the field"

Indicators

Warning flags

People in charge of key decisions about the initiative are not at all familiar with the socio-cultural reality in the area at stake

Percentage of local people who say they trust the staff of the conservation initiative and value their presence

Major complaints by local people about the attitude and behaviour of the staff of the initiative (either openly expressed or surfacing upon questioning)

The staff of the initiative know much less than local people about local conservation and social issues but still dictate the rules

Reports that staff are offering undue advantages to some local groups, or even aiding parties who undermine the initiative (e.g., poachers)

Number of activities that originated from suggestions made by stakeholders

3.4

Options for action

The following options for action offer some ideas on how the conservation initiative can deal with its most immediate social concerns — those of the people it employs. The options need to be considered in the light of particular circumstances, depending on which they may or may not be appropriate. You will undoubtedly think of other options as well. Importantly, the list of options for actions should not be viewed as a step-by-step procedure, although it is subdivided in the order in which options would be logically considered (for example, you may want to have internal meetings among staff before calling for meetings among staff and stakeholders). Also, some of the options below are alternatives to one another and need to be compared in terms of appropriateness to the particular context.

The list of options is subdivided into three groups according to the type of activity. These are:

Options to improve internal relationships among staff, and build upon their commitment and capacities

3.4.1	Staff review of internal management issues
3.4.2	Regular staff meetings to communicate and evaluate ongoing work
3.4.3	'On-the-job' capacity building
3.4.4	Decentralizing decision-making within the conservation initiative
3.4.5	Reviewing the initiative for timing and flexibility

Options to improve relationships among staff and local stakeholders

3.4.6	Hiring staff from local area
3.4.7	Staff visits to the field operations
3.4.8	Cultural presentations for the staff of the initiative
3.4.9	Integrating local culture and traditions within the conservation initiative

Options to sustain the relationship between the conservation initiative and the local stakeholders

3.4.10	Extraordinary staff and stakeholder meetings
3.4.11	Ongoing communication programme
3.4.12	Monitoring change in the local communities
3.4.13	Networking with local leaders and opinion-makers

Staff review of internal management issues

Appoint an individual or team from the staff, or set up a number of groups or committees to review the internal management policies regarding particular issues (e.g., hiring procedures, staff salaries, opportunities for professional advancement, internal communication, etc.). Tailor the size of the review team to match the size of the organization and the severity of the problem. Where there are tensions within the project team, it may be helpful to bring in a skilled outsider to facilitate the review process. Such a person should be able to look at the operations and structures more dispassionately and to raise issues which staff may feel uncomfortable in addressing.

Giving staff the responsibility of identifying not only problems but also solutions means that the proposed changes are likely to be 'owned' and therefore supported by the staff. For this reason, it maybe appropriate to involve all staff in some way in the review process.

It is important that the results of the review are fed back to the staff at large, and that they are all given the opportunity to respond to the recommendations. This ensures that staff members have the opportunity to check, and, if necessary, correct the interpretation of the information that each of them provided to the reviewer(s) before organizational changes are made.

It is also important that the reviewer(s) have sufficient seniority to deal with all the issues and levels within the organization. For instance, focusing just on solving administrative problems at the field level will not bring great benefits if the attitudes and practices of senior management are the key issues undermining the morale of the staff.

See Questions 3.2.1, 3.2.2 and 3.2.3, Volume 1; Concept Files 4.27 (A project or a process?) and 4.28 (Management styles), Volume 2; Planning, and Monitoring and Evaluation, in Section 5, Volume 2; and Example 43a in Section 6, Volume 2.

For further reference

Option for action 3.4.2

Regular staff meetings to communicate and evaluate ongoing work

Establish a regular schedule of staff meetings where people can discuss all the issues they care about (with the agenda to be set by all the staff). Make sure that time in the meetings is dedicated to updating colleagues on work carried out by individuals, and to ongoing evaluations of the effectiveness of activities. Make sure that the climate is appropriate for disagreements, discussion of alternatives and "replanning", as appropriate.

Staff meetings can be very effective in building a sense of team spirit and commitment among the project staff, from management to field technicians. The process encourages staff to think about the conservation initiative holistically rather than just about the particular aspect they are involved with.

Staff meetings also increase the chance that potential problems will be identified and dealt with before they damage the initiative. As with any meetings where problems/issues are identified, it is important to ensure that appropriate responses are decided, processes put in place, responsibilities allocated and agreed actions undertaken.

It is also important to watch out for boredom at meetings, and to prevent one or a few people monopolizing the floor for their own interests. The role of the chairperson in the meeting should rotate regularly to encourage a sense of shared responsibility among the staff.

For further reference

See Questions 3.2.4 and 3.2.6, Volume 1; Concept File 4.28 (Management styles), Volume 2; Planning, and Monitoring and Evaluation in Section 5, Volume 2; and Examples 44a-b in Section 6, Volume 2.

On-the-job capacity building

Option for action 3.4.3

Assign part of the management budget to training and professional enhancement of the staff. Make sure that staff identify areas where they face professional problems and suggest ways to enhance their capacities to respond to such problems. Encourage staff to present and analyze their field experiences as part of ongoing training.

On-the-job training has two major advantages over more formal courses. First, it is directed specifically at tasks required for the conservation initiative; second, the lessons learned can be directly experimented with and put into practice.

Providing staff with opportunities to increase their professional capacities will benefit the initiative through improved staff performance as well as through fostering a greater sense of staff loyalty and commitment.

It is important that staff are provided with training and professional enhancement opportunities that actually match the needs of the initiative. It is also important that there is no bias in the choice of staff being provided with capacity-building opportunities. Favouritism — perceived or actual — will damage staff relationships and team spirit as will the feeling that the training needs of some staff are being neglected because their roles within the initiative are not appreciated.

See Questions 3.2.3 and 3.2.6, Volume 1; and Examples 45a-e in Section 6, Volume 2.

For further reference

Option for action 3.4.4

Decentralizing decision-making within the conservation initiative

Make sure that as many staff as possible are empowered to make decisions at different levels within the management structure. In particular, this should apply to decisions directly related to each person's work, whether inside the agency or between the agency and the local community. This empowerment will make the organization more flexible and efficient in responding to needs as they arise, since decisions will be made closer to the on-the-ground issues. It will also give staff a greater sense of job satisfaction.

For decentralized decision-making to be successful, staff must have clear guidelines on the extent and limits of their authority and feel they are personally responsible and accountable for results to match that authority. They must also have adequate capacity and support to be able to make sound decisions and resist coercion from vested interests.

For further reference

See Questions 3.2.2 and 3.2.3, Volume 1; Concept Files 4.18 (Decentralizing and devolving government) and 4.28 (Management styles), Volume 2; and Examples 46a-c in Section 6, Volume 2.

Reviewing the initiative for timing and flexibility

Option for action 3.4.5

Carry out regular reviews of the conservation initiative, with particular focus on the timing of activities and the amount of flexibility allowed for ongoing replanning and responses to specific opportunities and problems. Check that the schedule is realistic, that the human resources are sufficient, and that all other resources required are available.

Conservation initiatives need to respond to change in the natural environment, as well as change in the availability of resources, people's priorities, technology, the political situation, etc. Regular reviews are a way of assessing progress and evaluating how to respond to such change. The reviews should be carried out on a regular basis (e.g., every six months) so that problems which could undermine the effectiveness and sustainability of the initiative are noticed and dealt with before they cause damage.

Involve representatives of the local community in the exercise and, if applicable, donor agencies as well. Involving the local people and donors will reinforce their sense of ownership and commitment to the conservation initiative.

See Questions 3.2.1 and 3.2.5, Volume 1; Concept File 4.27 (A project or a process?), Volume 2; Monitoring and Evaluation in Section 5, Volume 2; and Example 47a in Section 6, Volume 2.

For further reference

Option for action 3.4.6

Hiring staff from the local area

Hire people from the local area for jobs in the conservation initiative. Specifically consider technical and managerial positions, and not only support jobs. Give preference to people conversant with local language, culture and conditions who do not belong to political factions or parties which are in open conflict with some groups or sectors in the local society. Local staff should have contact with local stakeholders but, at the same time, be protected from pressures for undue favours.

This option offers an effective way of integrating local conservation skills and knowledge into the initiative, thus making it more sustainable in the long-term. It is also likely to result in a more stable staffing situation, especially in remote areas where outsiders are likely to take a position only for a limited period. Also, the employment of locals is the most efficient and effective way of reducing barriers between the initiative and the local community due to language and cultural differences. Employing local people can bring advantages to the local community as well. For instance, it ensures that at least a part of the salaries and wages is retained locally, as an immediate and tangible benefit of the initiative.

Staff selected on the basis of being locals must be locally well accepted. It is advisable to check out their history and standing in the community with key community members prior to making any appointment. For local staff, their level of credibility in the community is at least as important as their professional qualifications.

To avoid creating disparities in the local economy, ensure that pay rates and other benefits for local staff are aligned with those being paid in other local institutions. At the same time, ensure that differences between local and non-local pay rates are justifiable and accepted by the relevant staff.

For further reference

See Questions 3.2.5 and 3.2.6, Volume 1; Concept File 4.24 (Jobs in conservation), Volume 2; and Examples 48a-f in Section 6, Volume 2.

Staff visits to field operations

Option for action 3.4.7

Organize reasonably frequent field visits for all the professional staff involved in the initiative, including managers and administrators, to familiarize them with the area and meet the local stakeholders. If appropriate and possible, include the donors of the initiative as well.

It is advisable that some visits be well planned, but that others be made on the spur of the moment. The professional staff may wish to discuss beforehand what to look for and what they hope to learn, so that their observations and meetings will be focused and instructive. The team should strive to meet those people who are members of local decision-making groups such as Conservation Councils or major resource-user associations.

See Question 3.2.5 , Volume 1; and Examples 49a-b in Section 6, Volume 2.

For further reference

Option for action 3.4.8

Cultural presentations for the staff of the initiative

Organize meetings, presentations and shows for the staff of the conservation initiative (in particular, for non-local staff!) to learn about local history, cultural customs and beliefs, and existing or past institutions and systems for resource management. One approach that may be appropriate is to help the local people to make their own video/slide show, illustrating the environmental issues in their community and the aspects of their environment which are important to them. The video could record the development of the initiative and document environmental improvements and community responses over time. Provide ways of discussing the presentations together among staff and local people.

If appropriate, the 'cultural' sessions could provide a forum in which to consider how to deal with local customs that are at odds with conservation of local resources and/or with internationally recognized human rights.

For further reference

See Questions 3.2.5 and 3.2.6, Volume 1; Concept File 4.29 (Cross-cultural communication and local media), Volume 2; Social Communication, in Section 5, Volume 2; and Examples 50a-c in Section 6, Volume 2.

Integrating local culture and traditions with the conservation initiative

Option for action 3.4.9

Look for connections between traditional beliefs and values and the objectives of the initiative and develop these connections in the approach, objectives and information material of the initiative. Look for opportunities to expand and enhance positive traditional activities.

For example, dedicate some resources to collecting background information on traditional practices and activities. Discuss these in joint meetings between local people and staff. In agreement with the local people, record their stories and myths on conservation issues, and store them in ways that provide easy access (e.g., cassette tapes). Present the recordings to the community as a contribution from the conservation initiative.

See Questions 2.2.2 and 3.2.5, Volume 1; Concept Files 4.2 (Indigenous resource management systems), 4.10 (Local knowledge in conservation) and 4.11 (Indigenous people and protected areas), Volume 2; Information Gathering and Assessment, and Planning in Section 5, Volume 2; and Examples 51a-c in Section 6, Volume 2.

For further reference

Option for action 3.4.10

Extraordinary staff and stakeholder meetings

Whenever a decision must be made that will affect the local community in a significant way, organize a special meeting to discuss the reasons for the decision and its implications for staff and local stakeholders.

Ensure that the venue and time for the meeting are suitable for all parties. Conduct the meeting in a way that encourages an open discussion of pros and cons and, in particular, measures to reduce any detrimental impacts on stakeholders. Make sure that all the information needed for staff and stakeholders to understand the issue is available at the meeting and in a form which everyone can understand. As much as possible, those affected by the proposed change need to understand and accept the need for action.

The meetings can become a forum for resolving actual or potential conflicts among stakeholders or between stakeholders and the initiative. If this is a possibility, care should be taken in selecting a skilled facilitator. It may also be appropriate for the meeting to be chaired by an acknowledged and respected leader from the area.

For further reference

See Questions 3.2.1 and 3.2.5, Volume 1; Concept File 4.15 (Conflicts in conservation), Volume 2; Social Communication, and Conflict Management in Section 5, Volume 2; and Examples 52a-b in Section 6, Volume 2.

Ongoing communication programme

Assign to capable, experienced staff the task of maintaining ongoing relationships with local stakeholders and, in particular, assisting them in primary environmental care initiatives and other projects to generate benefits and economic returns from conservation.

For instance, relationships could be maintained by a regular series of events (such as a weekly or monthly radio programme, or a theatre group performing at ceremonies or local social occasions) in which people expect to hear news about the conservation initiative. Make the events as interactive as possible (accept calls from listeners, read out letters received, invite local speakers, ask the audience to comment, intervene in the scene, etc.).

A regular newsletter in the local language is another possibility. Make sure it is understandable by local people and addresses matters of interest to them. Involve local people in the preparation of the newsletter and other events, to enrich and 'test' the effectiveness of the chosen communication tools and avenues.

Adopt other systems of communicating information as appropriate to the area and the initiative. These could include pamphlets and posters; presentations to schools and churches; guided tours of the conservation area, etc. It is important that the methods used to communicate take into account the needs of those who are illiterate. In this sense, posters, guided tours and audio-visual displays are particularly appropriate, as well as presentations to groups.

Ongoing communication is important for the maintenance of trust between the parties. The links also facilitate a sharing of information and the prevention of conflicts. However, being 'in touch' is not enough. As issues arise, the management of the conservation initiative needs to respond to local concerns and take action as appropriate.

See Questions 1.2.6 and 3.2.5, Volume 1; Concept File 4.29 (Cross-cultural communication and local media), Volume 2; Social Communication in Section 5, Volume 2; and Examples 53a-c in Section 6, Volume 2.

For further reference

Option for action 3.4.12

Monitoring change in the local communities

Establish a system to monitor change in the status of local socio-economic conditions and relationships with the conservation initiative. Appropriate questions to address include: is there substantial change in the capacity of local people to meet their own needs? Is there substantial change in the impact on the ecosystem caused by local use of resources? Are there substantial changes in the attitudes of local people towards the initiative?

The monitoring system could form part of the ongoing participatory monitoring and evaluation programme, if one exists, or it could be a purely internal exercise for the benefit of management, based on field-worker reports.

For further reference

See Questions 2.2.1, 2.2.2, 2.2.3, 2.2.4, 2.2.5 and 3.2.1, Volume 1; Monitoring and Evaluation in Section 5, Volume 2; and Example 54a in Section 6, Volume 2.

Networking with local leaders and opinion-makers

Option for action 3.4.13

Organize a system (meetings, letters, telephone contact) of keeping local leaders and opinion-makers informed about the conservation initiative. Seek their input and advice as appropriate. This will reduce the possibility that they will resent the conservation initiative and use their influence to undermine its credibility.

Make sure that the individuals and organizations selected for networking are those which have the support of the local community. In some areas established traditional organizations may be more appropriate than new organizations with less credibility and relevance to local communities. In other areas the opposite may be true. There may also be conflicts of power between the old and new with each trying to establish or retain its power base. Consult with local people before assuming which organizations have the most relevance and usefulness to the management and implementation of the initiative. Strive to remain outside local power struggles.

See Question 3.2.5, Volume 1; Concept File 4.3 (Local institutions for resource management), Volume 2; and Example 55a in Section 6, Volume 2.

For further reference

General References

Agarwal, A. and S. Narain, *Towards Green Villages: A Strategy for Environmentally-sound and Participatory Rural Development*, Centre for Science and Environment, New Delhi, 1989.

Amend, S. and T. Amend, *National Parks Without People? The South American Experience*, IUCN, Gland (Switzerland), 1995 (also available in Spanish: *?Espacios sin Habitantes? Parques Nacionales de América del Sur*, IUCN Gland (Switzerland) and Nueva Sociedad, Caracas, 1992).

Anderson, K. and R. Blackhurst (eds.), *The Greening of World Trade Issues*, Harvester/Wheatsheaf, New York, 1992.

Asian Development Bank, *Guidelines for Social Analysis of Development Projects*, 1991.

Banuri, T., Hyden, G., Juma, C. and M. Rivera, *Sustainable Human Development*, UNDP, New York, 1994.

Banuri, T. and J. Holmberg, *Governance for Sustainable Development: A Southern Perspective*, IIED (International Institute for Environment and Development), London, 1992.

Barzetti, V. and Y. Rovinski (eds.), *Toward a Green Central America: Integrating Conservation and Development*, Kumarian Press, West Hartford (Connecticut), 1992.

Barzetti, V. (ed.), *Parks and Progress*, IUCN and Inter-America Development Bank, Washington D.C., 1993.

Bass, S., Dalal-Clayton, B. and J. Pretty, *Participation in Strategies for Sustainable Development*, IIED, Environmental Planning Issues No.7, London, 1995.

Berger, P. L., *Pyramids of Sacrifice: Political Ethics and Social Change*, Anchor Press, New York, 1974.

Berkes, F. (ed.), *Common Property Resources: Ecology and Community-based Sustainable Development*, Belhaven Press, London, 1989.

Biodiversity Conservation Network, *Studying the Social Dimensions of Biodiversity Conservation: Strategies, Approaches, Methods, and Resources*, manuscript draft, 1996.

Braatz, G., Davis, G., Sheen, S and R. Rees, *Conserving Biological Diversity: A Strategy for Protected Areas in the Asia-Pacific Region*, Technical Paper No. 193, World Bank, Washington D.C., 1992.

Bromley, D. W. and M. M. Cernea, *The Management of Common Property Natural Resources: Some Conceptual and Operational Fallacies*, World Bank Discussion Paper 57, The World Bank, Washington D.C., 1989.

Bromley, D. W., *Making the Commons Work: Theory, Practice and Policy*, ICS (Institute for Contemporary Studies) Press, San Francisco, 1992.

Brown, M. and J. McGann (eds.), *A Guide to Strenthening Non-governmental Organization Effectiveness in Natural Resource Management*, PVO-NGO/NRMS Project with USDA Forest Service, Washington D.C., 1996.

Brown, M. and B. Wyckoff-Baird, *Designing Integrated Conservation and Development Projects*, Biodiversity Support Program, Corporate Press, Landover (Maryland), 1994.

Bruce, J. W., *Legal Bases for the Management of Forests Resources as Common Property*, University of Wisconsin, Madison, 1996 (forthcoming).

Carbale, B., Rodriguez, J. and A. Salas, *Private Investment as a Mechanism for Sustainable Forest Development in the Americas*, World Resources Institute, Comisión Centroamericana de Ambiente y Desarollo and IUCN, San Pedro Sula (Honduras), 1995.

CEBSE/CANARI, *La Participación Comunitaria en la Gestión Ambiental y el Co-manejo en la República Dominicana*, CEBSE, Santo Domingo and CANARI, St. Lucia, 1994.

Centre for Science and Environment, *Protection of Nature Parks: Whose Business?*, Centre for Science and Environment, New Delhi, 1996.

Cernea, M. M., *Putting People First*, World Bank and Oxford University Press, New York, 1985.

Cernea, M. M., *Involuntary Resettlement in Development Projects: Policy Guidelines in World Bank-financed Projects*, World Bank Technical Paper 80, Washington D.C., 1988.

Cernea, M. M., *Using Knowledge from Social Science in Development Projects*, World Bank Discussion Papers 114, Washington D.C., 1991.

Chambers, R., *Rural Development: Putting the Last First*, Longman, London, 1983.

Chapin, M., *Mesoamérica*, Centro de Investigaciones Regionales de Mesoamérica y Plumsock Mesoamerican Studies, Vol. 16, issue 29, Guatemala, 1995.

Clay, J. W., *Generating Income and Conserving Resources: 20 Lessons From the Field*, WWF (World Wildlife Fund), Gland (Switzerland), 1996.

Dasmann, R. F., "The relationship between protected areas and indigenous peoples" in McNeely, J. and K. Miller (eds), *Proceedings of the World Congress in National Parks*, IUCN, Gland (Switzerland), 1983.

Davidson, J. and Myers, D. with M. Chakraborty, *No Time to Waste: Poverty and the Global Environment*, Oxfam, Wiltshire (UK), 1992.

Diegues, A. C., *O Mito Moderno da Natureza Intocada*, NUPAUB - Universidade de São Paolo, São Paolo, 1994.

Drijver, C., *People's Participation in Environmental Projects in Developing Countries*, IIED, Dryland Networks Programme Paper No.17, Centre for Environmental Studies, Leiden (The Netherlands), 1990.

Durning, A. B., *Action at the Grassroots: Fighting Poverty and Environmental Decline*, Worldwatch Paper 88, Washington D.C., 1989.

Fisher, R. J., *Collaborative Management of Forests for Conservation and Development*, Issues in Forest Conservation Series, IUCN and WWF, September 1995.

Forest, Trees and People Newsletter, Quarterly Newsletter from the FTP Programme networking activities.

Franke, R. W. and B. H. Chasin, *Seeds of Famine: Ecological Destruction and the Development Dilemma in the West African Sahel*, Allan Held Publishers, Montclair (New Jersey), 1980.

Friedmann, J. and H. Rangan (eds.), *In Defense of Livelihood: Comparative Studies on Environmental Action*, Kumarian Press, West Hartford (Connecticut), 1993.

Geoghegan, T. and V. Barzetti (eds.), *Protected Areas and Community Management*, Paper No. 1 in the Series 'Community and The Environment – Lessons from the Caribbean' by the Panos Institute and the Caribbean Natural Resources Institute (CANARI), Washington D.C., 1992.

Ghai, D. and J. M. Vivian (eds.), *Grassroots Environmental Action: People's Participation in Sustainable Development*, Routledge, London, 1992.

Gilmour, D. A. and R. J. Fisher, *Villagers, Forests and Foresters*, Sahayogi Press, Kathmandu, 1991.

Grassroots Development, Journal of the Inter-American Foundation.

Hannah, L., *African People, African Parks: An Evaluation of Development Initiatives as a Means of Improving Protected Area Conservation in Africa*, USAID, Biodiversity Support Program and Conservation International, Washington D.C., 1992.

Harrison, P., *The Third Revolution: Environment, Population and a Sustainable World*, Tauris, London, 1992.

Hoefsloot, H. and G. Onyango, "Seeking new approaches to forest conservation: Mount Elgon National Park", *SWARA*, Sept-Oct 1995.

IIED, *Whose Eden?: An Overview of Community Approaches to Wildlife Management*, Russel Press, Nottingham (UK), 1994.

ILEIA Newsletter, Publication of the Information Centre for Low-External-Input and Sustainable Agriculture (ILEIA) in Leusden (The Netherlands).

Inglis, J. T., *Traditional Ecological Knowledge: Concepts and Cases*, International Program on Traditional Ecological Knowledge, IDRC (International Development Research Centre), Ottawa, 1993.

IUCN, *World Conservation*, Quarterly Journal from IUCN, Gland (Switzerland).

IUCN/UNEP/WWF, *Caring for the Earth: A Strategy for Sustainable Living*, Gland (Switzerland), 1991.

IUCN, *Guidelines for Protected Area Management Categories*, IUCN and WCMC, Gland (Switzerland), 1994.

IUCN Commission on National Parks and Protected Areas (CNPPA), *Parks for Life: Action for Protected Areas in Europe*, IUCN, Gland (Switzerland), 1994.

IUCN Pakistan, *Proceedings of the Karakoram Workshop*, Skardu (Pakistan), September 28-29, 1994.

IUCN Uganda, *Proceedings of the Workshop on Collaborative Management of Protected Areas – Exploring the Opportunities in Uganda*, IUCN, 1996 (manuscript).

IUCN, *Best Practice for Conservation Planning in Rural Areas*, IUCN, Gland (Switzerland) and Cambridge (UK), 1995.

IUED (Institut Universitaire d'Etudes du Développement), *Guide d'Approches des Institutions Locales (GAIL): Méthodologie d'Étude des Acteurs Locaux dans le Monde Rural*, Itineraires, Notes et Travaux No. 40, Geneva (Switzerland), 1994.

Jackson, B. E. and A. Ugalde (eds.), *The Impact of Development and Modern Technologies in Third World Health*, Studies in Third World Societies, Publication Number 34, College of William and Mary, Williamsburg (Virginia), 1985.

Jodha, N. S., *Sustainable Development in Fragile Environments*, Environment and Development Series, Centre for Environment Education, Ahmedabad (India), 1995.

Kemf, E. (ed.), *The Law of the Mother*, Sierra Club Books, San Francisco, 1993.

Kiss, A. (ed.), *Living With Wildlife: Wildlife Resource Management with Local Participation in Africa*, World Bank Technical Paper 130, African Technical Department Series, The World Bank, Washington D.C., 1990.

Kitching, G., *Development and Underdevelopment in Historical Perspective: Populism, Nationalism and Industrialization*, Routledge, London, 1989.

Kleitz, G., *Frontieres des Aires Protégées en Zone Tropicale Humide*, GRET, Paris, 1994.

Kothari, A., Singh, N. and S. Suri, *People and Protected Areas: Towards Participatory Conservation in India*, Sage Publications, New Delhi, 1996.

Krishna G. and M. Pimbert (eds.), *Social Change and Conservation: Environmental Politics and Impacts of National Parks and Protected Areas*, UNRISD (United Nations Research Institute for Social Development), Geneva (Switzerland), 1996.

Liz Claiborne and Art Ortenberg Foundation, *The View from Airlie*, Results from discussions during the Community-based Conservation Workshop held in Airlie, Virginia, October 17, 1993.

Makombe, K, *Sharing the Land*, IUCN/ROSA Environmental Issues Series, 1, Harare, 1993.

Marks, S., *The Imperial Lion: Human Dimensions of Wildlife Management in Central Africa*, Westview Press, Boulder (Colorado), 1994.

Max-Neef, M. A., *From the Outside Looking In: Experiences in 'Barefoot Economics'*, Dag Hammarskjöld Foundation, Uppsala, 1982.

McCay, B. and J. M. Acheson, *The Question of the Commons: The Culture and Ecology of Communal Resources*, The University of Arizona Press, Tucson, 1987.

McNeely, J., "Assessing methods for setting conservation priorities", IUCN, Gland (Switzerland), March 1996.

McNeely, J., "Common property resource management or government ownership: improving the conservation of biological resources", *International Relations*, 10 (3), 1991.

McNeely, J. (ed.), *Expanding Partnerships in Conservation*, Island Press, Washington D.C., 1995.

McNeely, J. and K. Miller (eds), *National Parks, Conservation and Development: The Role of Protected Areas in Sustaining Society*, Smithsonian Institution Press, Washington D.C., 1984.

McNeely, J. and G. Ness, "People, parks, and biodiversity: issues in population-environment dynamics", IUCN, Gland (Switzerland), 1995.

Miller, K., *Balancing the Scales*, World Resources Institute, Washington D.C., 1996.

Murphree, M. W., *Communities as Resource Management Institutions*, IIED Gatekeeper Series No. 36, London, 1993.

Ndione, E. S., *Dynamique Urbaine d'une Société en Grappe*, ENDA, Dakar, 1987.

Oakley, P. et al., *Projects with People: The Practice of Participation in Rural Development*, International Labour Office, Geneva, 1991.

Ostrom, E., *Crafting Institutions for Self-Governing Irrigation Systems*, ICS (Institute for Contemporary Studies), San Francisco, 1992.

Pasos, R., Girot, P., Laforge, M. and P. Torrealba with D. Kaimowitz, *El Ultimo Despale*, FUNDESCA, San José (Costa Rica), 1994.

People and the Planet, journal published quarterly by Planet 21 and supported by IPPF, IUCN, UNFPA and WWF.

Picciotto, R. and R. Weaving, "A new project cycle for the World Bank", *Finance and Development*, December 1994.

Pimbert, M. P. and J. N. Pretty, *Parks, People and Professionals: Putting "Participation" Into Protected Area Management*, Discussion Paper 57, UNRISD-IIED-WWF, Geneva (Switzerland), February 1995.

Poffenberger, M., *Joint Management of Forest Land: Experiences from South Asia*, Ford Foundation, New Delhi, 1990.

Poffenberger, M. (ed.), *Keepers of the Forest*, Kumarian Press, West Hartford (Connecticut), 1990.

Poffenberger, M., *Grassroots Forest Protection: Eastern Indian Experiences*, Asia Forest Network, Berkeley (California), 1996.

Poffenberger, M., and B. McGean, *Village Voices, Forest Choices: Joint Forest Management in India*, Oxford University Press, New Delhi, 1996.

Poole, P., *Indigenous Peoples, Mapping, and Biodiversity Conservation*, Biodiversity Support Program and World Wildlife Fund, Washington D.C., 1995.

Poore, D. (ed.), *Guidelines for Mountain Protected Areas*, IUCN, Gland (Switzerland) and Cambridge (UK), 1992.

Pye-Smith, C. and G. Borrini Feyerabend with R. Sandbrook, *The Wealth of Communities: Stories of Success in Environmental Management*, Earthscan Publications, London, 1994.

Raju, G., Vaghela, R. and M. S. Raju, *Development of People's Institutions for Management of Forests*, VIKSAT, Ahmedabad (India), 1993.

Ralston, L., Anderson, J. and E. Colson, *Voluntary Efforts in Decentralized Management: Opportunities and Constraints in Rural Development*, Research Series No. 53, Institute of International Studies, University of California, Berkeley, 1983.

Read, T., *Coastal Resource Issues in Papua New Guinea: A Photo-text Collection*, Greenpeace, Boulder, 1994.

Read, T. and L. Cortesi, *Lessons from a Participatory Workshop*, Greenpeace, Boulder, 1995.

Reader, J., *Man on Earth*, Penguin Books, London, 1990.

Richards, P., *Indigenous Agricultural Revolution: Ecology and Food Production in West Africa*, Unwyn Hyman, London, 1985.

Roseland, M., *Toward Sustainable Communities: A Resource Book for Municipal and Local Governments*, National Round Table on the Environment and the Economy, Ottawa, 1992.

Ruiz, J. and R. Pinzón, *Reservas Extractivistas*, IUCN, Gland (Switzerland), 1995.

Russell, D., *Theory and Practice in Sustainability and Sustainable Development*, U. S. Agency for International Development (Center for Development Information and Evaluation), Washington D.C., 1995.

Sarkar, S., Singh, N., Suri, S., and A. Kothari, *Joint Management of Protected Areas in India*, Workshop Report, Indian Institute of Public Administration, New Delhi, 1995.

Saunier, R. E. and R. A. Meganck (eds.), *Conservation of Biodiversity and the New Regional Planning*, Organization of American States, Washington and IUCN, Gland (Switzerland), 1995.

Schoeffel, P., "Cultural and institutional issues in the appraisal of projects in developing countries: South Pacific water resources", *Project Appraisal*, Vol. 10, No. 3, September 1995.

Scoones, I. and J. Thompson (eds.), *Beyond Farmer First: Rural People's Knowledge, Agricultural Research and Extension Practice*, Intermediate Technology Publications, London, 1994.

Slocombe, S., Roelof, J. K., Cheyne, L. C., Noalani Terry, S. and S. den Ouden, *What Works: An annotated bibliography of case studies of sustainable development*, IUCN-CESP Working Paper No. 5, International Center for the Environment and Public Policy, Sacramento (California), 1993.

Society for the Promotion of Wasteland Development (SPWD), *Joint Forest Management: Concepts and Opportunities*, SPWD, New Delhi, 1992.

Solis, V., Cabrera, J. and T. Tuomasjukka, *Biodiversidad: Su Tratamiento en Centroamérica*, Fundación Ambio, San José (Costa Rica), 1995.

Stahl, M., *Constraints to Environmental Rehabilitation Through People's Participation in the Northern Ethiopian Highlands*, Discussion Paper 13, UNRISD, Geneva (Switzerland), 1990.

Steiner, A. and E. Rihoy, "The commons without the tragedy?", background paper for the 1995 Regional Conference of the Natural Resource Management Programme, USAID, Malawi, 1995.

Stiefel, M. and M. Wolfe, *A Voice for the Excluded. Popular Participation in Development: Utopia or Necessity?*, Zed Books, London and UNRISD, Geneva (Switzerland), 1994.

UNESCO, *Biosphere Reserves: The Seville Strategy and the Statutory Framework of the World Network*, UNESCO, Paris, 1996.

UN (United Nations), *Population, Environment and Development*, Proceedings of the United Nations Expert Group Meeting on Population, Environment and Development, United Nations Headquarter, 20-24 January 1992, United Nations, New York, 1994.

UNDP (United Nations Development Programme), *Conserving Indigenous Knowledge*, UNDP, New York, 1994.

Uphoff, N., *Local Institutional Development: An Analytical Sourcebook with Cases*, Kumarian Press, West Hartford (Connecticut), 1986.

Ventocilla, J., "Kuna Indians and the Conservation of the Environment" *Mesoamérica*, Vol. 16, issue 29, Centro de Investigaciones Regionales de Mesoamérica, Guatemala, 1995.

Weber, J., "L'occupation humaine des Aires protegées à Madagascar: diagnostic et éléments pour une gestion viable", *Natures, Sciences, Sociétés*, 3, Vol. 2: 157-164, 1995.

Wells, M., Brandon, K. and L. Hannah, *People and Parks: Linking Protected Area Management with Local Communities*, World Bank, WWF and USAID, Washington D.C., 1992.

West, P. C. and S. R. Brechin, *Resident Peoples and National Parks*, University of Arizona Press, Tucson (Arizona), 1991.

Western D., and R. M. Wright (eds.), *Natural Connections: Perspectives in Community-based Conservation*, Island Press, Washington D.C., 1995.

White, A. T., Zeitlin H. L., Renard, Y. and L. Cortesi, *Collaborative and Community Based Management of Coral Reefs: Lessons from Experience*, Kumarian Press, West Hartford (Connecticut), 1994.

Wild, R. G. and J. Mutebi, *Conservation Through Community Use*, UNESCO, 1996 (in press).

Wolfson, M., *Community Action for Family Planning: A Comparison of Six Project Experiences*, OECD, Paris, 1987.

Contributors

Institutional partners

International Union for the Conservation of Nature (IUCN), Social Policy Group

Biodiversity Support Program (BSP), a USAID funded consortium of the WWF, the Nature Conservancy and the World Resources Institute

The World Bank, Social Policy and Resettlement Division

PVO-NGO/NRMS Project (managed by World Learning, CARE and WWF)

World Wildlife Fund, United States (WWF-US), Social Science and Economic Programme

Center for International Forestry Research (CIFOR)

Intercooperation, Switzerland

Project coordinating committee

Janis Alcorn, Director, Asia and Pacific, BSP

Grazia Borrini-Feyerabend, Head, Social Policy Group, IUCN

Michael Brown, Director, PVO-NGO/NRMS Project

Gloria Davis, Chief, Social Policy and Resettlement Division, The World Bank

John Krijnen, Intercooperation

Patricia Larson, Director, Social Science and Economic Programme, WWF-US

Eva Wollenberg, Senior Scientist, CIFOR

Consultants and interns

Dianne Buchan, New Zealand

Roger Ebner, Switzerland

Sally Jeanrenaud, Switzerland

Peter-John Meynell, UK

Paul Sochaczewski, Switzerland

Patrizio Warren, Italy

Layout, graphic work and publishing support

Appi S.à r.l., Switzerland

Dhunmai Cowasjee, IUCN Pakistan

Patricia Halladay, Canada

Saneeya Hussein, IUCN Pakistan

Ajmal Malik, Intercooperation Pakistan

Fabrizio Prati, Switzerland

Morag White, IUCN

Computer support

Dan Hinckley, IUCN

Fayez Mikhail, IUCN

Secretariat Support

Susan Broomfield, Social Policy Group, IUCN

James-Christopher Miller, BSP

Nathalie Pannetier, Social Policy Group, IUCN

Participants of start-up workshop at IUCN

Carmen Aalbers, International Labour Organization

Solon Barraclough, United Nations Research Institute for Social Development

Jill Blockhus, Forestry Conservation Programme, IUCN

Grazia Borrini-Feyerabend, Social Policy Group, IUCN

Montserrat Carbonell, RAMSAR Bureau

Hin Keong Chen, Asia and Pacific Affairs, IUCN

Charles Crothers, University of Kent, Australia

Peter Crowley, International Save the Children Alliance

Khrisna Ghimire, United Nations Research Institute for Social Development

Donald Gilmour, Forest Conservation Programme, IUCN

Paddy Gresham, Environmental Assessment Services, IUCN

Meghan Golay, Social Policy Group, IUCN

Peter Hislaire, Africa Desk, IUCN

Mark Hufty, Institut Unversitaire d'Etudes du Développement, Geneva

Sally Jeanrenaud, Consultant, Switzerland

John Krijnen, Intercooperation, Switzerland

Kevin Lyonette, Director Government Aid Agencies Relations, WWF International

Gayl Ness, Social Policy Group, IUCN

Raewyn Peart, University of Kent, Australia

Maria Petrone-Halle, Medecins sans Frontières, Switzerland

Pedro Rosabal, Protected Areas Programme, IUCN

Per Rydèn, Acting Assistant Director General, IUCN

Patrizio Warren, Consultant, Italy

Contributors of case study material/comments

Carmen Aalbers, International Labour Organization

H. R. Akanda, Local Government Engineering Department, Dhaka, Bangladesh

Janis Alcorn, BSP

Kirsten Ewers Andersen, Project RAMBOLL, Denmark

Ivannia Ayales, Consultant, Costa Rica

Siddharta Bajracharya, Annapurna Conservation Area Project, Nepal

Demba Baldé, Senegal Office, IUCN

Tom Barton, Consultant, Uganda

Katrina Brandon, Consultant, USA

Michael Brown, PVO-NGO/NRMS Project

John Butler, WWF US

Gabriel Campbell, The Mountain Institute, USA

Paul Chatterton, South Pacific Program, WWF

Carol Colfer, Consultant, CIFOR

Maria (Chona) Cruz, Social Policy and Resettlement Division,
The World Bank

Dulan de Silva, Pakistan Office, IUCN

Carole Donaldson, Landcare, New Zealand

Charles Doumenge, Central Africa Office, IUCN

Eduardo Fernandez, Social Policy Group, IUCN

Gonzalo Flores, PROBONA, Bolivia

Pascal Girot, University of San José, Costa Rica

Markus Gottsbacher, International Labour Organization

Peter Hislaire, Regional Support Group, IUCN

Hartmut Holzknecht, Research School of Pacific and Asian Studies,
Australia

Ashish Kothari, Indian Institute of Public Administration, India

John Krijnen, Intercooperation

Patricia Larson, WWF-US

Juan Mayr, Fundacion Pro-Sierra Nevada de Santa Marta, Colombia

Jeffrey McNeely, Biodiversity Program, IUCN

Katherine McPhail, Social Policy and Resettlement Division,
The World Bank

Alice Mogwe, DITSHWANELO, Botswana

James Murombedzi, Center for Applied Social Sciences, University of
Zimbabwe

Marshall Murphree, Centre for Applied Social Sciences, University of
Zimbabwe

Jackson Mutebi, CARE, Uganda

Samuel-Alain Nguiffo, Centre pour l'Environement et le
Développement, Cameroon

Aijaz Nizamani, Pakistan Office, IUCN

Antonio Perez, Consultant, Spain

Pauline Peters, Yale University, USA

Adrian Phillips, Commission on National Parks and Protected Areas,
IUCN

Lynelle Preston, The Mountain Institute

Esther Prieto, Centro de Estudios Humanitarios, Paraguay

Muhammad Rafiq, Pakistan Office, IUCN

Jean-Richard Rakotondrasoloarimanana, COMODE, Madagascar

Elizabeth Reichel, Universidad de los Andes, Colombia

Catherine Roffet, Consultant, France

Per Ryden, acting Asst. Director General Conservation Policy, IUCN

Lea Scherl, Consultant, Nairobi

Maria Cristina Serje de la Ossa, ECOFONDO, Colombia

Evelyn Silva, Fundación Ecotropica, Costa Rica

Peter Valentine, James Cook University, Australia

Michael Vardon, Wildlife Management International, Australia

Katherine Warner, RECOFTC, Thailand

Grahame Webb, Wildlife Management International, Australia

Eva Wollenberg, CIFOR

Contributors of Concept Files

Anil Agarwal, Director, Centre for Science and Environment, India

Janis Alcorn, Director, Asia and Pacific, BSP

Grazia Borrini-Feyerabend, Head, Social Policy Group, IUCN

Michael Brown, Director, PVO-NGO/NRMS Project

Gerardo Budowski, Professor, University of Peace, Costa Rica

Michael Cernea, Senior Advisor for Social Policy and Sociology, The World Bank

Carol Colfer, Consultant, CIFOR

Alex de Sherbinin, Social Policy Group, IUCN

Bob Fisher, Senior Lecturer in Development Studies, University of West Sydney, Australia

Donald Gilmour, Head of Forest Conservation, IUCN

Pascal Girot, Professor, University of Costa Rica

Roy Hagen, Shapeaurouge, Minnesota (USA)

Narpat Jodha, National Resource Management Specialist, Social Policy and Resettlement Division, The World Bank

Aban Marker Kabraji, Country Representative, Pakistan Office, IUCN

Ashish Kothari, Senior Lecturer, Indian Institute of Public Administration, India

Larry Kohler, Focal Point for Environment and Social Development, ILO

Connie Lewis, Associate Director, The Keystone Centre, Colorado (USA)

Rowan Martin, Chair, IUCN Africa Sustainable Use Initiative, Zimbabwe

Jeffrey McNeely, Chief Scientist and Head of Biodiversity Conservation Group, IUCN

Marshall Murphree, Director, Centre for Applied Social Sciences, University of Zimbabwe

Gayl Ness, Social Policy Group, IUCN

Elinor Ostrom, Co-director, Workshop on Political Theory and Policy Analysis, Indiana University, (USA)

Mark Poffenberger, Asia Forest Network

Yves Renard, Executive Director, Caribbean Natural Resources Institute

Ricardo Ramirez, Coordinator, Information and Communication, ILEIA, The Netherlands

Martha Rojas, Biodiversity Conservation Group, IUCN

Dianne Russell, Biodiversity Conservation Network, The Philippines

Paul Sochaczewski, Consultant, Switzerland

Barry Spergel, Legal Advisor for Conservation Finance, WWF-US

Peter Valentine, Senior Lecturer Tropical Environment Studies, James Cook University, Australia

Frank Vorhies, Biodiversity Conservation Group, IUCN

Anoja Wickramasinghe, University of Peradeniya, Sri Lanka

Eva Wollenberg, Senior Scientist, CIFOR

Barbara Wyckoff-Baird, WWF, Namibia

Contributors of supplementary material and advice

Lorena Aguilar Revelo, IUCN-ORMA, Costa Rica

Yati Bun, FSP, Papua New Guinea

Daniele Cassin, EDEX, Italy

Christian Châtelain, Conkouati Project, IUCN Congo

Moreno Chiovoloni, Consultant, Rome

Marcus Colchester, World Rainforest Movement, England

Lafcadio Cortesi, Greenpeace, USA

Sandy Davis, Social Policy and Resettlement Division, The World Bank

Nelson Dias, Guinea-Bissau Office, IUCN

Biksham Gujja, WWF, Switzerland

Ursula Hiltbrunner, Membership Unit, IUCN

Henk Hoefsloot, Mt Elgon Project, IUCN Uganda

Chris Horill, IUCN Tanga Project, Tanzania

Ruud Jansen, Botswana Office, IUCN

Elizabeth Kemf, WWF International

Nancy MacPherson, Environmental Strategy Group, IUCN

Rob Monro, Zimtrust, Zimbabwe

Michel Pimbert, WWF Switzerland

Gert Polet, Nigeria Office, IUCN

Tom Price, Niger Office, IUCN

Charlie Pye-Smith, Journalist, United Kingdom

Jorge Rodriguez, Consejo Centroamericano de Bosques y Área Protegidas, Costa Rica

Alberto Salas, IUCN-ORMA, Costa Rica

Richard Sandbrook, IIED, UK

Neena Singh, Centre for Science and the Environment, India

Vivienne Solis, IUCN-ORMA Costa Rica

Achim Steiner, Washington Office, IUCN

Mario Tapia, University of Lima, Peru

Ibrahim Thiaw, Regional Support Group, IUCN

Cécile Thiery, Information Management Group, IUCN

Jim Thorsell, World Heritage Programme, IUCN